T0208849

DID YOU KNOW?

DID YOU KNOW?

Over One Hundred Facts about Haiti and Her Children

MARJORIE CHARLOT

DID YOU KNOW?
OVER ONE HUNDRED FACTS ABOUT HAITI AND HER CHILDREN

iUniverse books may be ordered through booksellers or by contacting:

iUniverse
1663 Liberty Drive
Bloomington, IN 47403
www.iuniverse.com
1-800-Authors (1-800-288-4677)

Because of the dynamic nature of the Internet, any web addresses or links contained in this book may have changed since publication and may no longer be valid. The views expressed in this work are solely those of the author and do not necessarily reflect the views of the publisher, and the publisher hereby disclaims any responsibility for them.

Any people depicted in stock imagery provided by Thinkstock are models, and such images are being used for illustrative purposes only. Certain stock imagery © Thinkstock.

ISBN: 978-1-4917-7690-2 (sc)
ISBN: 978-1-4917-7692-6 (hc)
ISBN: 978-1-4917-7689-6 (e)

Library of Congress Control Number: 2015916610

Print information available on the last page.

iUniverse rev. date: 11/17/2015

Contents

To God and my ancestors—thank you.

And to my people, in the words of Joseph Auguste Anténor
Firmin in *De l'Égalité des Races Humaines* (*The Equality of
Human Races*), may this book "inspire in all of the children of
the black race around the world the love of progress, justice, and
liberty. In dedicating this book to Haiti, I bear them all in mind,
both the downtrodden of today and the giants of tomorrow."

Acknowledgments

To several colleagues who read and helped with each draft of this book without complaint and gave helpful suggestions and words of encouragement. The author is also very grateful to the army of proofreaders, especially Desiree Rucker, who helped with not only proofreading but also editing. Thank you all.

Introduction

Did you know …?

The world knows about the Haitians' great achievement of 1804, the year they defeated three major world powers (France, England, and Spain) for their independence. It was an accomplishment that amazed and frightened the world at the same time. If this feat had been the work of European men, it would have been heralded to this day for the military genius it displayed. At the least, Haiti's hard-won freedom would be spoken of with the respect and reverence given to the right of every man to fight against tyranny, the creed to which their captors theoretically paid homage. Did you know that even America's first president, George Washington, a slave owner, sided with the French slave owners? As repayment for funds loaned to American revolutionaries during the Revolutionary War, France requested that $400,000 in emergency assistance be given to the slave owners of St. Domingue. Upon hearing their pleas for help, Washington authorized then secretary of state Thomas Jefferson (also a slave owner) to send the French slave owners $40,000 in emergency relief as well as one thousand weapons. Even Venezuela gave $400,000 in aid to Napoleon's fruitless bid to recapture Haiti.

The American revolutionaries had snatched America out of the hands of England, their own mother country, over what they considered an onerous tax burden. The Haitian people dared to fight their oppressors who had stolen many of them from their native lands, dehumanized them, and worked them to death. By declaring themselves equal to the men of Europe, the freedom fighters of Haiti had made lifelong enemies.

Based on the silence about the history of Haiti, one would believe that once freed from the oversight of their colonial masters, the Haitians retired to the shade of their palm trees and sat on their laurels. This would explain the poverty and desperation that has the world proclaiming Haiti as the poorest country in the northern hemisphere. Hard work, in fact, is not the issue, as the Haitian people work tirelessly to eke out a living. While Haiti suffers from extreme poverty economically, most people don't know that when the French finally resigned to their fate as losers, they imposed an ordinance requiring Haiti to pay 150 million francs and provide a 50 percent tariff reduction for all French ships docking in Haiti. The fledgling government of Haiti borrowed the full amount of the first payment of 30 million francs from a private French bank, MM Ch Ternaux Grandolphe et Cie. Though once one of the most prosperous colonies, the free black republic of Haiti was encumbered by debt at its birth and surrounded by rich and powerful racist enemies hoping for its downfall.

One cannot understate the turmoil that has plagued Haitian politics. Since its independence, Haiti has had various government systems. During the aristocracies, there were two emperors, Jean-Jacques Dessalines in 1804 and Faustin Soulouque, and one king, Henri Christophe. Democracy rule was the ideal; however, during democracies there were numerous coups, with two president assassinations. Two dictatorships (presidents-for-life Major Sylvain Salnave and the Duvalier family) masquerading as democracies were painful periods in Haiti's past. The people of Haiti struggle to this day for a just, democratic government. There should be no question as to whether Haitian men and women are courageous. Haiti has a history of military intervention, and Haiti fought for American independence during the American Revolution and with the French against Spain in the Spanish-American War. They even offered to fight with America in WWII against the Nazis. Did you know that Haitians were integral members of the Tuskegee Airmen?

Not just fighters, Haitians are artists, writers, engineers, architects, and entrepreneurs. The canon of literature would be poorer if *The Three Musketeers* and *The Count of Monte Cristo* had not been written by Alexandre Dumas, Père. This excellence is a legacy for the writers Jacques Roumain, author of *Gouverneurs de la Rosée* (*Masters of the Dew*); Marie Vieux-Chauvet, novelist, poet, playwright, and author of *Amour, Colère et Folie* (*Love, Anger, Madness*); and most recently, Edwidge Danticat, the award-winning novelist. Rodney Leon, the celebrated architect and designer of the African Burial Ground Monument and the Ark of Return Memorial at the United Nations

Headquarters in New York City, is also of Haitian descent. Visual artists of note abound, and there is the stunningly beautiful metal work of Haitian sculptors known as Fè Koupé that is in collections around the world. Much of the genteel charm of New Orleans (the wrought ironwork and housing style) is due to the Haitian architects and builders who migrated from Haiti when the French were ousted. Interestingly, these Creoles were fleeing the new black republic.

The media has stereotyped Haitians as typically migrating to the United States as boat people. Surprisingly, in 1723, a group of black Haitians were among the first nonnative people to settle in Missouri. The sheer nonsense and misrepresentation of the Haitian people that has been circulated in the press must be countered. One must fight lies with facts, and this is what I have set out to do. In addition, while researching this book, I happened upon information that was a revelation to me and might be to you as well. However, this book does not claim to contain every fact worth knowing, and it is my intention to update the information at least every two years.

The contributions that the nation of Haiti and her children who are dispersed throughout the world have made to western civilization will never be accurately counted. This is not only due to omission but also to the fact that many people of Haitian descent consider themselves Spanish or French, as in the case of Jorge Biassou, whose real name is Georges Biassou, a Haitian freedom fighter who later became a Spaniard. There are many African Americans who are of Haitian descent who are not even aware of their Haitian heritage.

I have used subject categories to list within these pages just a few of the notable, and dare I say, in some instances, great contributions by Haiti's known descendants. This book will give you an expanded view of Haiti and the people who hail from her shores. You will understand why I am extremely proud of the country of my heritage and why I am honored to be a Haitian.

Salutations,

Marjorie Charlot

1

Basic Facts about Haiti

Name:
Repiblik Dayiti—in Kréyòl
République d'Haiti—in French
Republic of Haiti—in English

Capital:
Port-au-Prince

Ayiti: the original name of Haiti, given by the Arawak people, that means "mountainous land." It would appear that the natives of Ayiti also referred to their country as *Bohio* and *Quisqueya* (translation "large land"[1]).

1492: Haiti was "discovered" by Christopher Columbus on December 6, 1492, and he named it Espanola (in English, Hispaniola), which means "Little Spain." On Christmas of the same year, the *Santa Maria* sank off the coast of Haiti.[2]

Haitian Population 2015:[3]
9,996,731

Ethnic Groups:
95 percent blacks
5 percent mulatto and white

Official Languages:
Creole (Kréyòl)—spoken by 90 percent of the Haitian population[4]
French

Religion:[5]
Roman Catholic 80 percent, Protestant 16 percent (Baptist 10 percent, Pentecostal 4 percent, Adventist 1 percent, other 1 percent), none 1 percent, other 3 percent.

Territory and Geography:
Haiti comprises a total area of 10,714 square miles (27,750 square km), an area slightly larger than the state of Maryland. Haiti is the western third of the island of Hispaniola, which is the second largest island in the Caribbean. It is located between the Caribbean Sea and the north Atlantic Ocean. Haiti shares Hispaniola with the Dominican Republic. Haiti's landscape has towering mountains ranges, interspersed with fertile lowland plains and lakes.[6]

Climate:
Haiti is a tropical country with variations in weather depending on elevation.

National Anthem:
"La Dessalinienne" is the national anthem of Haiti. It was written by Justin Lhérisson (1872–1907), composed by Nicolas Geffrard (1871–1930), and adopted in 1904.[7]

Natural Resources:
Bauxite, copper, calcium carbonate, gold, marble, and hydropower.[8]

Currency:
Gourde (HTG)

Holidays:
Independence Day—January 1
National Heroes' Day or Ancestors' Day—January 2
Carnaval—February
Agriculture and Labor Day—May 1
Mother's Day—May 25
Mother's Day—May 11 (American date)

Many Haitians celebrate Mother's Day on both dates.
Flag Day—May 18
Jean-Jacques Dessalines Day (anniversary of his death)—October 17
All Saints' Day—November 1
Day of the Dead—November 2
Anniversary of the Battle of Vertières (last major battle for independence)—November 18
Christmas—December 25

2

Chronology

Spanish Rule (1492–1697)

1492: Haiti is "discovered" by Christopher Columbus on December 6, 1492. He names it Espanola (in English, Hispaniola), which means "Little Spain."

1493: Indigenous population consists of 200,000 to 300,000 Arawaks. When Columbus returns to Hispaniola, he brings with him mastiffs, greyhounds, and attack dogs to terrorize the Arawaks/Tainos.

1494: The first uprising of the natives takes place.

1496: Arawak population is decimated to one-third. Santo Domingo is established by Spanish settlers.

1502: The first group of enslaved Africans of Spanish descent called Ladinos are brought to Haiti by Spanish governor Nicolás de Ovando.

1505: Sugarcane cultivation is introduced to Hispaniola.

1516: Bishop Bartolomé de las Casas suggests to the Spanish Crown that Africans should replace the natives as slaves.

1520: African slaves are used throughout the colonies. The slaves from West Africa, called *bozales*, are the slaves of choice because they are considered more docile than Ladinos.

1521: A group of Bozales plan and organize the first major slave rebellion on Hispaniola and prove that they are far from docile by killing several Spaniards. The twenty or so Bozales who started this rebellion are the property of Diego Colón, who is the governor of the island and the son and heir of Christopher Columbus.

1530: Only a few hundred Arawak are left alive.

1600s: The French, English, and Dutch take over the northern and western coasts of the island. Many of these new settlers are outlaw pirates called buccaneers.

1625: The first French settlements on Tortuga Island, off the northwest coast, are established.

1641: French buccaneers establish settlements in northwestern Hispaniola.

French Rule (1679–1804)

1679: Slave Padrejean leads the first slave revolt in Port-de-Paix, St. Domingue.

1697: The French acquire the western third of Hispaniola with the Treaty of Ryswick and name its new colony Saint Domingue.

1750s: The plantation system on St. Domingue grows rapidly, and by the 1750s it is the leader in sugar production, producing more sugar than all of Britain's West Indies colonies combined. France controls roughly 40 percent of the worldwide sugar trade and 60 percent of its coffee trade. St. Domingue's slave population is 500,000 or almost half of the total slave population in the Caribbean. France's current economic growth and industrial development is due to the labor of the blacks in St. Domingue.

1758: François Makandal (born in Guinea), one of the most famous revolutionary Maroons in the history of Haiti, became legendary among both blacks and whites in St. Domingue. Makandal and his men start a twelve-year-long rebellion against whites in St. Domingue by attacking plantations at night, burning them down and killing their owners. While planning a major attack, he is betrayed and caught. Makandal is executed on January 20, 1758. His execution takes place in a public square in Cap Francais, today known as Cap Haitian.

1760: France begins widespread coffee cultivation in Haiti.

1767: St. Domingue's annual exports reach $140 million, dwarfing that of the thirteen American colonies and even that of Spain's colonies. This figure corresponds to 123 million pounds of sugar, one million pounds of indigo, and two million pounds of coffee, along with animal hides, molasses, coca, and rum. By 1789, there are one thousand merchant ships carrying goods between St. Domingue and France. This represents the percent of all French export and import trade.

1770: Port-au-Prince is made the colonial capital by the French. On June 3, an earthquake hits Port-au-Prince.

1777: Treaty of Aranjuez delineates a boundary between French and Spanish colonial territory in Hispaniola.

1779: The Siege of Savannah occurs.

1788: Société Amis des Noirs (Society of the Friends of Blacks) is founded by Jacques-Pierre Brissot de Warville. The society advocates for the abolition of the slave trade.

1790: Mulattoes, led by Ogé and Jean Baptiste Chavannes, start a rebellion in northern St. Domingue. Ogé's army of rebels number only 250–300.

1790s: The net worth of the colony is put at $300 million. The island consists of 792 sugar plantations, 2,180 coffee plantations, 705 cotton plantations, 3,097 indigo plantations, 69 cocoa plantations, and 632 subsistence crops.

1791–1803: The slaves of St. Domingue launch a rebellion led by a Creole slave born in Jamaica named Dutty (or Zamba) Boukman. This insurrection becomes a war that lasts for thirteen years. Haitians not only fight Napoleon's army but also Spanish and British forces that assisted the French.

1796–1801: Toussaint Louverture comes into power.

1801: Toussaint Louverture defeats the British and Spanish troops that invaded Santo Domingo. Slavery is abolished in Santo Domingo.

1803: On May 18, the Haitian flag is created by Catherine Flon, who is the goddaughter of Jean Jacques Dessalines, in the city of Archaie. Dessalines orders that the phrase "Freedom or Death" be inscribed on the blue and red flag. The Battle of Vertières marks the ultimate victory of the former slaves over the French.

Independence (1804)

1804: On January 1, in the western city of Gonaïves, General Jean-Jacques Dessalines declares Haiti's independence from the French. The country is officially named Ayiti (Haiti in English), an Arawak word meaning "mountainous land."

1805: Dessalines promulgates Haiti's first constitution. Henri Christophe begins construction of the Citadel.

1806: Emperor Jean-Jacques Dessalines is assassinated. The leaders of this assassination are Alexandre Pétion and Henri Christophe.

1807: Henri Christophe is proclaimed president of the state of Ayiti, Alexandre Pétion is declared president of the Republic of Ayiti, and another civil war breaks out.

1810: Christophe begins construction of Sans-Souci.

1811: Christophe crowns himself King Henri I.

1818: Alexandre Pétion dies without naming a successor. Jean-Pierre Boyer, who was Pétion's secretary and friend, is declared president for life.

1820: Christophe takes his own life. On October 26, Boyer reunites Haiti.

1821: President Boyer invades Santo Domingo following its declaration of independence from Spain. The entire island is now controlled by Haiti until 1844.

1825: France, threatening to re-enslave Haitians, imposes an ordinance requiring Haiti to pay 150 million francs and provide a 50 percent tariff reduction for all French ships docking in Haiti. To meet the first payment of thirty million francs under the terms of the ordinance, the government of Haiti borrows the full amount from a private French bank, MM Ch Ternaux Grandolphe et Cie.

1838: Under the Traité d'Amitié (Treaty of Friendship), the original obligation of 150 million francs is reduced to ninety million francs, with the government of Haiti required to make thirty annual payments of two million francs in order to pay off the balance of sixty million francs. However, in addition to these terms, Haiti is still liable for paying the onerous interest rates of the original obligation to France.

1862: The United States finally grants Haiti diplomatic recognition, sending abolitionist Frederick Douglass as its consular minister.

1904: "La Dessalinienne" is adopted as Haiti's national anthem.

Occupation of Haiti (1915)

1915: One hundred and eleven years after the successful slave revolt, some 80 percent of the Haitian government's resources are being paid to French and American banks on loans that had been made to enable Haiti's reparations to France.

President Woodrow Wilson orders the US Marines to occupy Haiti and establish control over customs, houses, and port authorities. The Haitian National Guard is created by the occupying Americans. The marines force peasants into *corvée* labor, building roads.

1916–1924: Americans occupy the Dominican Republic.

1919: US Marines assassinate *cacos* (guerrilla fighters) leader Charlemagne Masséna Péralte.

1922: Seven years into a nineteen-year American military occupation of Haiti, which resulted in fifteen thousand Haitian deaths, the United States imposes a loan of $16 million on the Haitian government to pay off its "debt" to France.

1934: The United States withdraws from Haiti, leaving the Haitian military in control.

After the Occupation (1934)

1937: Dominican dictator Rafael Trujillo orders the execution of Haitians, which results in the killing of 17,000 to 35,000. This is known as the Parsley Massacre.

1947: The American loan is finally paid off. Haiti is left virtually bankrupt, its workforce in desperate straits. The Haitian economy never recovers from the financial havoc France (and America) wreaked upon it during and after slavery.

1957: Dr. Francois "Papa-Doc" Duvalier declares himself president for life and forms the paramilitary Tonton Makout. During his dictatorship, tens of thousands of Haitians are killed or exiled.

1971: Nineteen-year-old Jean-Claude Duvalier becomes president for life after the death of his father, Dr. Francois "Papa-Doc" Duvalier.

1986: Duvalier and his family are exiled to France after widespread protests.

1990: Ertha Pascal-Trouillot is named the provisional president of Haiti from 1990 until 1991. She is the first woman in Haitian history to hold that office.

1991: Ex-Catholic priest Jean-Bertrand Aristide takes the oath of office as the fortieth president of Haiti. He is elected president with 67.5 percent of the popular vote.

1995: Claudette Werleigh makes history as Haiti's first female prime minister.

2004: Aristide leaves office under pressure of an armed rebellion by a rebel group calling itself the Revolutionary Artibonite Resistance Front. The group is led by Guy Philippe, a former police chief.

2008: Michèle Pierre-Louis becomes prime minister of Haiti. She is the second female prime minister in Haiti's history.

2010: On January 12, Haiti is hit by a catastrophic magnitude 7.0 Mw earthquake, followed by at least fifty-two aftershocks. The earthquake causes an estimated 300,000 deaths, displaces more than a million people, and damages nearly half of all structures within the epicenter area, which includes Haiti's capital, the city of Port-au-Prince.

2011: Michel Martelly is elected president, winning 68 percent of the vote in a runoff election.

2014: Jean-Claude Duvalier dies in Port-au-Prince, Haiti, at the age of sixty-three. He had returned to Haiti in January 2011.

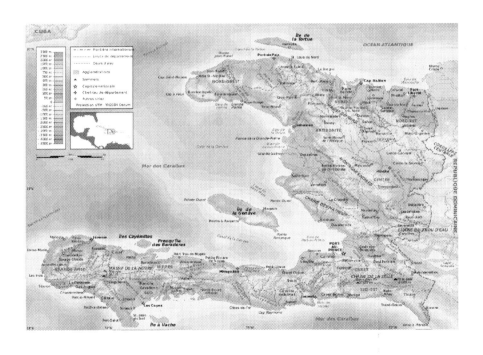

3

The Natives of Haiti

The pencil of God has no eraser.
—Haitian proverb

The history of the Arawak/Tainos of Haiti is both fascinating and tragic. Haiti at one time was inhabited by three different groups of natives, the first being the Guanahatabey (Ciboneys) around AD 450, and the second the Arawaks or Tainos around the seventh or eighth century, an agriculturalist group that originated from the Orinoco and Amazon basins. The third group was the Caribs, who came from South America and arrived in 1492 at the eastern tip of the island. It was after this third group of natives that the Caribbean Sea and region were named.[9]

Haiti was divided into five kingdoms, each of which was ruled by a *cacique* or chief. There was no decimation against genders, as both men and women could be a cacique. The five kingdoms at the time of Columbus's landing were as follows:[10]

- **Maguá** meant Kingdom of the Plain, and its plain was, according to Catholic priest Bartolomé De Las Casas, one of the wonders of the world. It extended some eighty leagues, right from the southern coast to the northern shore of the island, and was five to eight leagues wide. Its cacique was Guarionex.[11]
- **Marién** was a very rich region larger than Portugal. It was fertile and better suited for human inhabitation, and it produced gold and copper mines. A cacique named Guacanagarí ruled this kingdom.[12]

- **Maguana** was a beautiful and fertile region that enjoyed one of the healthiest climates. Maguana produced the best sugar of all of Ayiti. Its great cacique was Caonabo,[13] and his kingdom was the wealthiest of the five kingdoms.[14]

- **Xaraguá** was the heart and core of Ayiti. The language of this kingdom was refined, it had many nobles and great lords, its people were described as handsome and easy on the eyes by Las Casas, and its leading family was numerous and liberal. The cacique of this kingdom was Behechio, and his sister Anacaona became queen after his death.[15]

- **Higuey** was ruled by Queen Higuanama, who was already advanced in age when the Spaniards hanged her.[16] Countless people of her kingdom were killed. Some were burned alive while various others had their legs and arms cut off.[17]

The Arawak/Tainos society was divided into two classes: the *nitaíno* and *naboria*. The nitaíno were sub-chiefs, priests, and medicine people while the naboria essentially made up the working class. The society can be described as peaceful and nonviolent; if they did fight, it was most likely in self-defense. The people the Spaniards encountered were happy and friendly. The report of the Caribs being "fierce" and "warlike" or cannibals was fabricated by Columbus, who in reality neither visited any Carib island nor produced any evidence to support his claims. These lies were used to portray the Caribs as savages that needed to be tamed.

Housing and Craftsmanship

The population lived in organized villages in homes that were spacious, clean, and sturdily built, which was a surprise to the Europeans, who were accustomed to the charnel rows of hovels in large sections of their cities and villages.[18] There were two types of native home designs: the *caney*, which was the more popular of the two structures, was round-shaped, and the *bohío*, with its rectangular form, may have been influenced by the Europeans.

Houses were grouped around a central plaza, with the cacique's home being the largest, better made than the rest, and situated on the plaza. Family members all lived together in one big open space. As for furniture, some caciques slept on a wooden platform, but most people slept in *hamacas* (hammocks) made of cordage.

Food and Agriculture

One of the great achievements of the Arawaks/Tainos was their agricultural system, which included mounded fields called *conucos.* These mounded fields were knee-high and packed with leaves that prevented soil erosion. The crops that were planted in these conucos were yucca (sometimes called manioc), *batatas* (sweet potato), various squashes, and beans, creating a multicrop harmony. The conucos' design and crop choices guaranteed something would grow, no matter the weather conditions. American geographer Carl Sauer stated their agriculture was "productive as few parts of the world," and it gave the "highest returns of food in continuous supply by the simplest methods and modest labor … The white man never fully appreciated the excellent combination of plants that were grown in conucos."[19]

The native diet also consisted of fish, maize (corn), peppers, and peanuts.[20] Around their homes, they grew fruits, calabashes, cotton, and tobacco. They also cultivated pineapple.[21] In fact, much of the food in the Haitian and Dominican diets came from the Arawak/Tainos. For example, in Haiti, people still eat *casaba*, known in the Kréyòl (Creole) language as *kasav*, and maize is called *mayi*. In the Dominican culture, casaba is still known by this name, and the flour from it is called *catibias*. Like the natives, kasav today is also an important part of the diet of Haitians.[22]

Religion

The Arawaks/Tainos worshipped many deities, known as *zemis*, and two supreme deities were Yúcahu and Atabey. Yúcahu was the lord of cassava and the sea where the Arawaks/Tainos received their sustenance. Atabey was the mother of Yúcahu, the goddess of fresh water and human fertility. Native women who wanted a safe childbirth prayed to her.[23] The less important zemis were spirits of ancestors and those believed to live in nature, such as trees, rocks, and so forth. Individuals would keep their zemis in niches or tables, while caciques kept theirs in a separate house that resembled their own homes and was used as a temple.[24] Other zemis include the following:

- **Baibrama** was from the Classic Arawak/Tainos period. Natives would go to him for help in growing cassava and curing individuals poisoned by its juice. Baibrama is often depicted in a standing or squatting position with an erect penis, as if urinating to increase the growth of crops.[25]
- **Boinayel**, the Son of the Grey Serpent, was a rain god.[26]
- **Márohu** was considered the deity of fair weather; this may be because his name means cloudless. He is at times shown with his twin, Boinayel.[27]

Transportation

The form of transportation used by the natives of Ayiti was a *canoa* (canoes). These canoas were hollowed-out logs that could hold, according to Columbus's report, up to 150 people. Before the Spaniards introduced sails, spade-shaped paddles were used. The largest canoas were for the caciques. They were carved and painted, and the Arawaks/Tainos stored them in special boathouses reminiscent of those in Polynesia. Besides canoa, caciques, while on land, traveled in *litters*, which were used only by the caciques.[28]

The Genocidal End of the Arawak/Taino Natives

The native population of Haiti in 1492, before their extermination, could have been near eight million. Due to diseases and murder, the population was completely wiped out. The Arawak/Taino people of Haiti were a peaceful group who met these new foreigners to their land with courtesy that they soon would regret; unfortunately, they would not receive the same treatment in return from the Spaniards and were about to be exposed to the lowest level man could reach with regard to cruelty. The brutality under the Spaniards was so great that the natives took to killing themselves. One way they would accomplish this was by drinking the poisonous juice of the casaba. After delivery, mothers would kill their babies so they would not be enslaved. The country of Ayiti would become the first in the New World to be destroyed and depopulated by Christians.[29] Today, the Arawaks/Tainos, along with the Caribs, live in the blood of the present-day population of the Caribbean, as well as in their memories. Their culture is present today in various ways that many of us are unaware of, such as in some of the words we use and the food we eat.

4

The Africans

The child of a tiger is a tiger.
—Haitian proverb

The history of Haiti is one that is steeped in glory, corruption, terror, and conflict. Sadly, this legacy from the past continues today. The first person to bring blacks as slaves to Hispaniola was Nicholás de Ovando in 1502. These slaves came from West Africa. However, Bishop Bartolomé de Las Casas was the one who recommended the importation of African slaves to the New World because they were fitter for hard labor than the native population. De Las Casas suggested this to the royal family of Spain in 1516 because the size of the native population was decreasing under the cruelty they faced from the Spaniards, a suggestion the king of Spain took to heart, for by 1521, African slaves could be found throughout the colonies. Bishop Bartolomé de Las Casas opened the doors to a new form of genocide in the New World known as the transatlantic slave trade.

Although it is hard to imagine today, considering Haiti is a third-world country, but at one time, it was called the "Pearl of the Caribbean" because it was once the richest island in the Caribbean. This was due in part to the slaves who were worked to death, for in 1767, Saint-Domingue exported 123 million pounds of sugar, one million pounds of indigo, two million pounds of coffee, and along with this were animal hides, molasses, coca, and rum. By 1789, there were one thousand merchant ships carrying goods between Saint-Domingue and France, making up 67 percent of all French export and import trade.[30] In fact, the labor of Saint-Domingue blacks produced a combined annual export and import trade of $140 million, dwarfing that of the thirteen American colonies and even that of Spain's colonies.[31] In addition, in 1791, there were 792 sugar plantations, as well as 2,180 coffee, 705 cotton, 3,097 indigo, 69 cocoa, and 632 raising subsistence crops. Saint-Domingue's exports to France alone totaled approximately $41 million, with the net worth of the colony put at $300 million according to Heinl and Heinl in their text *Written in Blood*. It is no wonder that with all this money being made in France, the common saying was "rich as a Creole."[32] Planters made so much money in Saint-Domingue they were called the "Lords of Haiti" while planters on Martinique were called "Gentlemen of Martinique," and those in Guadeloupe were known as the "Good People of Guadeloupe." This great feat of production and wealth was possible because human beings were being worked to death. In Haiti, one-third of the slaves would die a few years after their arrival, just to be replaced by another group of slaves. They were easy to replace, for unlike the Spaniards who only had an island to plunder human souls, the French, on the other hand, as with the rest of Europe, had an entire continent to plunder. For example, according to Ros, in 1791, the number of slaves stood at a minimum of 450,000 and a maximum of 500,000. Every year, four thousand ships delivered at least thirty thousand new blacks from Africa, but there were also years when between fifty thousand and a hundred thousand were delivered.[33]

The Haitian Revolution was essentially inspired by the French Revolution. Haiti's fight for independence started on the night of August 22, 1791, and the leader of this rebellion was a Creole slave born in Jamaica named Dutty (or Zamba) Boukman, who, after his death, would be replaced by the great leaders of Haiti's war of independence: Toussaint Louverture, Henri Christophe, Jean Jacques Dessalines, and Alexandre Pétion. Many are aware that Haitians fought France for their freedom; however, not many know that Haiti also fought off the British and the Spanish during this struggle. Both of these countries wanted to control the Pearl of the Caribbean. The loss the British faced in Saint-Domingue would be one of the greatest disasters in British imperial history.[34] As for the Spanish who wanted their old colony back, they met their defeat under the leadership of Louverture. Dessalines, the tiger of Haiti, was also instrumental, aiding Toussaint in keeping both the British and Spanish forces at bay.[35] Haitian independence was won, thanks in part to the leaders mentioned above and the five hundred thousand slaves and maroon fighters, on January 1, 1804.

Unfortunately, freedom was not enough to shake the yokes of greed, corruption, and conflict. The history of Haiti is littered with tragedy and disaster, such as slavery, disease, genocide, injustice, oppression, dictatorship, occupation, wars, poverty, natural disasters, and most recently the earthquake of 2010.

5

Architecture and Monuments

1. Did you know ... part of the walls of the mountaintop fortress Citadelle Henri Christophe, known as Citadelle Laferrière, the largest fortress in the western hemisphere, was built at night by Henri Christophe, who was a skilled stonemason?[36]

2. **Shotgun house.**

Examples of Haitian adherence to African traditions in arts and culture can be found in objects as seemingly commonplace as the shotgun houses of New Orleans, Louisiana. These houses were erected in substantial numbers in Faubourg Tremé, an African American neighborhood near the French Quarter and are attributed to the mass immigration to the city of political refugees of Haitian descent from Cuba in 1809. Architectural historians credit this type of structure to design concepts native to the Yoruba, a people of Nigeria. These houses featured rooms in a straight line from the door off the street. The houses, designed to encourage air flow, featured high ceilings, large windows, and ventilation straight through the house. Examples of this style of architecture can still be found in Faubourg Tremé to this day.

3. **New Orleans ironwork.**

The massive influx of people from Saint Domingue contributed to the survival of numerous West and Central African cultural traditions. The decorative iron balconies that distinguish French Quarter architecture originated in an early New Orleans industry that flourished with the training of enslaved blacksmiths. Many adapted readily to European metal-forging techniques since ironworking was an ancient

West African technology. Slave artisans crafted the altar rails and doors of St. Louis Cathedral, as well as the gate of the Cabildo. By 1831, Afro-Creole New Orleans ironworkers, both enslaved and free, held a virtual monopoly on the trade. According to folk historians, highly skilled slave ironworkers who had been brought from Saint Domingue crafted wrought-iron railings in a French Quarter blacksmith shop on St. Louis Street.[37]

Citadelle Henri Christophe, known as Citadelle Laferrière (photo by SPC Gibran Torres, United States Army)

4. **Charles Philip Lazarus** "rose from humble beginnings to be the most prominent iron foundry in the island [Jamaica] in the second half of the nineteenth century."[38] He was born in Kingston, Jamaica, on May 1, 1836 to Marie Francis, a Haitian, and Abraham Lazarus. It was to his mother that Charles accredited his later success. He wrote this about her:

[She] was a black woman not possessing education, but she was very wise and extremely industrious. Her character was strong and determined and she had great self-respect. The counsel, advice and direction that she gave me from the very beginning of my life were of inestimable value to me. She was very shrewd. She would say to me, "My son, don't trouble to go as clerk although it may seem more attractive at first. Learn a trade and master it well; they will need you; they must have you." She encouraged me to make myself thorough and reliable, to use my time to the best advantage, to improve my mind.

His father, however, stopped taking care of him once he turned twelve years old, even though it was recorded that in 1840 Abraham Lazarus owned seventy-two acres of land at Mount Pleasant, St. Andrew. At twenty-four, Lazarus's education ended, and his working career began.[39]

In 1849, he was indentured to learn the plumbing trade. By nineteen, he had his own business, establishing his famous foundry in West Kingston in 1855. It is from this foundry that Lazarus trained over one thousand men. He also helped lay ocean telegraph cable, a job in which he was recognized for his skills. A year later, he cast a large water wheel for Savoy Estate in Clarendon. Lazarus also built the synagogue on Duke Street in 1888, which was later destroyed in an earthquake in 1907. One of his great accomplishments was the building of the famous George Stiebel's Devon House. Lazarus served on the Kingston City Council, which was just one of his various public activities. When he died in 1917, the editor of the *Jamaican Times* wrote the following about him:

Charles P. Lazarus was a personality of strong and distinctive character, cast in some respects on antique lines, which recalled at times a combination of the Roman and Puritan outlook on life. He was an original and stimulating thinker, possessing great powers of reflection, a luminous native wit and a large store of sound practical wisdom. With the spirit of thoroughness and efficiency he was imbued through and through, and his unerring instinct for essentials was a remarkable trait.[40]

5. **Rodney Leon** is a world-renowned architect. He designed the African Burial Ground National Monument, the first of its kind in New York City. The design, constructed of granite, stone, and water, was opened on October 5, 2007 at a cost of over $50 million.[41]

Leon is one of two cofounders of AARRIS Architects PC (the other founder is Nicole Hollant-Denis). According to the AARRIS Architects' website, Leon's educational background includes a degree from Pratt Institute School of Architecture in 1992 and a master's of architecture from Yale University in 1995.[42] Leon was one of five designers selected from sixty-one applicants to an initial call for proposals for the burial ground in 1998. According to the US General Service Administration, "In June 2004, National Park Service convened the five finalist's designers for a series of public forums in New York City's five boroughs. The finalists presented their designs for public comment and each designer revised their designs based on public feedback from these presentations."[43] In the end, it was Leon's design that was chosen. Of his design, Leon said the following:

My design tells the story and speaks to the greatness of a people who never ceased to push for freedom. Their story began in Africa, and the origin of my design was born there too. By traveling to Africa and incorporating the shapes and forms, as well as the essence of the culture and people, I have created a *living memorial* to the ancestors and their stories.[44]

He also stated the following:

The memorial represents a unique opportunity and responsibility for all of us. No longer will one walk past this site or through lower Manhattan, and not be provided the opportunity to know, understand and acknowledge and respect the significance of this site.[45]

6. **Skilled craftsmen**. Due to the influx of immigrants from Saint Domingue, it was only natural that they modeled their new homes on those they left behind. As many carpenters, masons, and inhabitants were Saint Dominguans, they have significantly influenced the architecture of Louisiana and South Carolina. Even today, in cities like Charleston and New Orleans, one can see buildings that resemble old buildings in Cape Haitian, which was known as Cap Français during colonial times. [46]

7. **Engineering aptitude**. According to "Rebuilding Haiti in the Martelly Era," 13 percent of African American engineers are of Haitian origin.[47]

Example of New Orleans ironwork (photo by M. Charlot)

African American Burial Monument (photo by M. Charlot)

6

Art and Culture

1. **Patrick H. Reason** was "a freeman born of Haitian immigrants, who was sponsored by the Anti-Slavery League to study engraving in England. Upon his return, he gained recognition as an illustrator of antislavery subjects and a portrait draftsman of important abolitionists. His most memorable work was the illustration for the antislavery slogan, 'Am I not a man and a brother?'"[48] He was the brother of Charles L. Reason.[49] (See "Education" chapter.)

2. **James Weldon Johnson** was a political activist, writer, and lyricist of popular songs, black musical theater, and the black national anthem "Lift Every Voice and Sing." (His brother J. Rosamond Johnson wrote the music.) Johnson's mother, Helen Louise Dillet, was a free woman of Haitian descent, who was born in Nassau, in the Bahamas, on August 4, 1842.[50]

3. **Sidney Poitier** was the first black to win an Oscar. "The Poitiers traced their name to the West Indian nation of Haiti … Reginald Poitier's slave ancestors had worked on sugar plantations in Haiti and then escaped to the Bahamas …"[51]

4. **Maxwell** is an R&B singer who is half-Haitian from his mother's side and half-Puerto Rican from his father's side. He lives in Brooklyn, New York. His full name is Gerald Maxwell Rivera.[52]

5. **Wyclef Jean** is a Haitian-born musician and record producer. He was a former member of the hip-hop group Refugee Camp (Fugees) that included Lauryn Hill and Prakazrel "Pras" Michel, Jean's cousin.

6. **Jean Michel Basquiat** was a Haitian American painter. He was born on December 22, 1960 in Brooklyn, New York. His father,

Gerard Basquiat, was born in Port-au-Prince, Haiti, and his mother, Matilde, was born in Brooklyn of Puerto Rican parents. On April 12, 1988, Basquiat died of a heroin overdose at the age of twenty-seven. His work has been exhibited throughout the world and is now in the collection of major owners and galleries.[53]

7. **Garcelle Beauvais** is a model-turned-actress and was voted one of "The Ten Sexiest Women" of 2001 by readers of *Black Men* magazine. She was born in Haiti, the youngest of seven children.[54]

8. **Quddus** is a Canadian MTV VJ and interviewer and former host of the MTV show *Total Request Live*.[55] His father is Haitian. Quddus's full name is Benjamin Quddus Philippe.

9. **Tyrone Edmond** is a model who was born in Cap-Haitian, Haiti. His full name is Enoch Edmond.[56]

10. **Meta Golding** is a Haitian-American actress who was born in India to a Haitian mother and American father. She has starred in various TV shows, and as of 2015, she is starring in *Tomorrow People*. Golding has also had movie roles in films such as *The Chicago 8* and *The Hunger Games*, wherein she plays knife-wielding warrior Enobaria. She is a Cornell University graduate and a world traveler, and she has lived in India, Haiti, Italy, Senegal, and France. Golding is a woman of many talents, for she not only speaks Italian, French, Creole, and English, but she also used to be a competitive figure skater. She frequently visits Haiti, where she has family.[57]

7

Beauty Pageant Winners

1. **Evelyn Miot,** Miss Haiti, was the first black woman to reach the semifinals in the Miss Universe pageant in 1962.[58]

2. **Gerthie David,** Miss Haiti, known as "The Black Goddess," is the second black woman to place first runner-up in the Miss Universe pageant in 1975 in San Salvador. She became a symbol to Haitian youth.[59]

3. **Joelle Apollon,** Miss Haiti World, came in sixth place at the Miss World 1975 pageant in London.[60]

4. **Marjorie Judith Vincent** is the daughter of Haitian immigrants. She was crowned Miss America in 1991, becoming the fourth African woman to win this title. She used her platform to help with the cause of domestic violence. Ms. Vincent, a classically trained pianist, graduated from DePaul University in Chicago with a degree in music in 1988. In 1994, she received a degree in law from Duke University in Durham, North Carolina. She later became a news anchor at WGBC-TV, an NBC affiliate station in Meridian, Mississippi.[61]

5. **Lisa Drouillard,** a Haitian American, was crowned Miss Teen New York in November 2010. According to the *New York Daily* newspaper, there had not been a Miss Teen USA from New York in nearly thirty years.[62] On June 14, 2011, Miss Drouillard was crowned Miss New York Teen USA.[63]

6. **Sarodj Bertin** was born in Port-au-Prince, Haiti. She was crowned Miss Haiti Universe on May 16, 2010 in Port-au-Prince. She speaks four languages: Creole, French, English, and Spanish. She is the daughter of Mireille Durocher Bertin, a prominent Haitian lawyer,

social leader, and human rights activist who was murdered in Port-au-Prince on March 28, 1995. Her mother was an outspoken critic of then president Jean-Bertrand Aristide. Like her mother, Miss Bertin is also a lawyer.[64]

8

Civil Rights

1. **Mary Ellen Pleasant** is considered the mother of civil rights in California. Nearly one hundred years before there was a Rosa Parks, there was Mary Ellen Pleasant, who fought to ride the trolleys of San Francisco. In 1863, she sued and won the rights for blacks to ride the trolleys. This case is known as *Pleasant v. North Beach & Mission Railway*. She was born in 1817 near Augusta, Georgia, the daughter of a Haitian slave and a Virginia governor's son. Pleasant, an ex-slave, worked the Underground Railroad, amassed a business fortune, and gave everything she had to find jobs and justice for her people.[65]

She married James W. Smith, a mulatto landowner-merchant and spy for William Lloyd Garrison's abolitionist newspaper, and joined her husband in his work in the Underground Railroad. She would dress as a black jockey to get onto plantations. After her husband's death, she married John James Pleasant but continued rescuing slaves out of bondage until she was found out and forced to flee. She fled to New Orleans, where she studied voodoo under Mme. Marie LaVeaux, who taught her a method of gathering and using personal secrets of the rich to leverage aid to the poor. Later she joined John Brown's mission to free slaves.[66]

After leaving New Orleans, she moved to San Francisco where she took on two identities to avoid being captured. One identity was that of Mrs. Ellen Smith, and she worked at a boarding house for white people. As Mary Pleasant, she would hire ex-slaves in her own businesses, which included a tenant farm, dairy farm, laundries, bordellos, livery stables, and a money-lending business. She was quite successful in "her investment in quicksilver mining and silver/ gold exchanges and amassed a $30 million fortune for her and her silent partner, Scotsman Thomas Bell." She lost some of her fortune with the decline in price of precious metals. She was known as Mammy Pleasant.[67]

2. **Charles L. Reason** (See "Education" chapter.)

9

Education

1. **W. E. B. Du Bois** was a great scholar and civil rights leader who helped establish the NAACP and was of Haitian descent. Dubois's grandfather, Alexander, lived in Haiti from about 1821 to 1830. While there, he married a Haitian woman and had a son, Alfred, (Dubois's father) who was born in 1825. The Haitian family that Alexander married into may have been the family of Elie Dubois, the great Haitian educator.[68]

2. **Dr. Carole M. Berotte Joseph** became the first Haitian American to head a US community college on March 1, 2005. She was the fourth president of Massachusetts Bay Community College (MassBay) in Wellesley Hills, Massachusetts, and was the first female president in this college's history. Dr. Joseph has a "bachelor's degree in Spanish with minors in French and education from York College, CUNY; a Master's in Education, with specializations in curriculum and teaching from Fordham University; an Advanced Certificate in Administration and Supervision from New York University and a Doctorate in Sociolinguistics and Bilingual Education from the Department of Teaching and Learning at New York University."[69] She speaks four languages: Haitian Creole, French, English, and Spanish.[70] Dr. Joseph achieved another first when, in January 2011, she was "appointed as President of Bronx Community College, becoming the first Haitian-born person to lead a campus in the City University of New York system."[71]

3. **Charles L. Reason** was born in New York on July 21, 1818 to Michiel and Elizabeth Reason, immigrants from Haiti who arrived in the United States shortly after the Haitian Revolution of 1793.[72] He was the first African American to teach at a predominantly white college, Free Mission College (later renamed New York Central College) in 1849. Reason was professor of *belles lettres*, Greek, Latin, and French and was an adjunct professor of mathematics at Central College.[73] After leaving Central College, he went on to the Institute for Colored Youth in Philadelphia and became principal. Under his leadership, he "increased student enrollment, expanded the library holdings and exposed the students to outstanding African American intellectuals and leaders of that time."[74] After three years, Reason left his post at the Institute for Colored Youth and returned to New York to become an administrator of schools in New York City. While there, he led the fight in 1873 to end racial segregation in the city's public schools.[75] He was the brother of engraver Patrick H. Reason. (See "Art and Culture" chapter.)

4. **Patrick School of Pharmacy** in Boston was "in the first half of the twentieth century one of the country's outstanding pharmaceutical schools. Its founder, Dr. Thomas W. Patrick, was born in Haiti in 1872 and educated in Trinidad; most of his students were white. An alumnus of his school was the first person to be granted a pharmacist's license by the Massachusetts Board of Registration. Dr. Patrick was known internationally and his school trained a good number of American pharmacists."[76] He operated his school until 1936, and his school trained approximately five thousand pharmacists.[77]

10

Explorers and Settlers

1. In 1723, a group of black Haitians and others become the first group of nonnative people to settle in Missouri. A group of five hundred black Haitians were sent to this American state to work in the mines. The mining proved to be unsuccessful, and many of these Haitians were employed in other occupations in Missouri and Iowa. Some were bought by French settlers, and the offspring of these Haitians formed a sizable portion of the slave population of Illinois.[78] Haitians were also among the first Wisconsin settlers. Jesuits there and in Illinois used them as farmers, blacksmiths, carpenters, brewers, and masons. They would mix with the Pawnee Indians, who also became slaves. In fact, the name "Pawnee" (Pani) came to be synonymous with "slave." Oshkosh, Wisconsin, was named after Oshkosh, a great Indian chief who was a descendent of these Haitian settlers. His son-in-law, John DuBe (DuBay), was described as a "black Ethiopian."[79]

2. **Jean Baptiste Pointe Du Sable** was the founder of Chicago. He was an explorer, fur trader, and farmer. He was educated in France. Du Sable spoke French, Spanish, English, and several native languages fluently. He was born in St. Marc, Saint Domingue, now known as Haiti. His father was a French captain, and his mother an enslaved black. A letter written by a British officer in 1779 described him as a handsome, well-educated French-speaking black man. No one had any idea what he looked like. Du Sable married a Potawatomi woman named Kittihawa, who later was renamed Catherine after converting to Catholicism. They had a son, Jean, and a daughter, Marie-Suzanne. It appears the name Chicago is linked to him: "In 1779, du Sable left Peoria to explore Eschikagou, or 'Fetid Swamp,' so named for its malodorous waters. In French, he rendered the name "Checagou," "Chicagot," or "Chicageaux." Later, English speakers

standardized the spelling to "Chicago."[80] He settled in the area, at head of the Chicago River, becoming the first settler. He built the city's first permanent home, where the Tribune Tower now stands. In 1796, one of his grandchildren was born, becoming the first child born in this settlement. There are various spellings of his name, including Pointe du Sable, Point de Sable, Point au Sable, Sabre, Saible, and so on.[81]

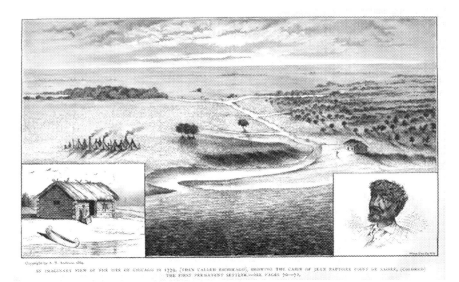

The cabin of Jean Baptist Du Sable

3. **Jan (Juan) Rodrigues** was a seafarer of African descent from Hispaniola (now Haiti and the Dominican Republic). He was part of the crew of the *Jonge Tobias* when the ship arrived at Manhattan Island. He was abandoned there in 1613. Soon after, he developed trade with the natives and even married a native woman from Rockaway, and they had several children. Rodrigues become one of the first middlemen in the early Amerindian-European trade. He helped European mariners negotiate with the natives. In return for his services, they paid him a commission.[82] Rodrigues became the first non-Native American settler of New York when he settled on

what is now known as Governor's Island, just off Manhattan in New York Bay.[83]

4. La Seccion de Los Americanos.

In 1825 during the rule of General Boyer of Haiti, hundreds of African-Americans went to settle in Santo Domingo, which was then under Haitian rule. Their descendants are still there and live principally at Santa Barbara de Samana in their own quarter, which is known as "La Seccion de Los Americanos." They have preserved their customs and their language.[84]

5. First settlers of Jamestown.

Africans, along with the Spaniard Lucas Vásquez de Ayllón, were the first to settle what is today Jamestown, Virginia in the early 1500s and he was the first to bring Africans into what is now the United States. Ayllón founded San Miguel de Guadalupe, a colony that flourished until 1527, when Ayllón died and was replaced by a more repressive ruler. Eventually the Africans rebelled, burning the settlement and forcing the Spanish to retreat to Haiti. Many of the Africans who fled the Spanish settlement established their own colony in the area. One could say, then, that this community of Africans was, after those of the Native Americans, the first permanent colony in Virginia.[85]

(See "Military, Revolts, Revolutions, and Wars" chapter.)

11

Great Families of Haitian Descent

The Dumas Family

1. **General Alexandre ("Alexandre the Greatest") Dumas** was born in Haiti on March 25, 1762, the son of Marie Cosette Dumas, an African woman of St. Domingo (Haiti), and the marquis Antoine Alexandre Davy de la Pailleterie, who was from an ancient Norman family. They named him Thomas Alexandre Davy de la Pailleterie.[86] The marquis de la Pailleterie was bored with life at court and went to St. Domingo where he settled in Jeremie and may or may not have married Marie Cosette Dumas; they were together for eleven years. Dumas's mother died when he was around ten, and eight years later his father returned to France, taking Alexandre with him.[87] He was educated at Bordeaux and was the talk of Paris.[88] Dumas was very dark, stood six feet two, and had incredible physical strength. He was a great swordsman, beating all except another Negro, Chevalier de St. Georges, who was also from the West Indies. Dumas was part of Saint-Georges's "colored regiment."[89] He was dubbed the greatest by Anatole France, who was fascinated by stories about Dumas.[90]

After his father remarried, Dumas's objection to this marriage resulted in him leaving his father's home. The marquis's words to him before he left were, "I have but one request, young man. Do not take my name around with you to dishonor it." He dropped his father's name and rejected his title. He took the name of his mother and became Alexandre Dumas. A few days later on June 2, 1786, he enlisted in the Army of the Rhine. It was around this time that he married Marie Labouret, the daughter of a hotelkeeper, before going to war again.[91]

In July 1786, he was promoted to brigadier general, and by September 3, he was a general. Five days later, he was appointed commander of the Army of the West. All of this occurred within the span of two years.[92] In the service, his strength came in handy. For example, once he and his men met the enemy, who were well defended by a palisade. Seeing that his men had trouble scaling the obstruction, he picked them up by the seat of their pants and started flinging them over the wall, which shocked the Austrians, who fled in horror, for it was literally raining men.[93] Another example of his bravery and strength was at a bridge at Brixen, which he was defending. In this battle, during which he killed eight and wounded several others, his men arrived just in time to save him. In this fight, Dumas suffered several wounds: three to the head, thigh, and arm; numerous small cuts; eight bullet holes; and his horse was killed.[94] This event earned him the title of "Horatius Cocles of the Tyrol" from Napoleon.[95]

Dumas's bravery showed itself again when he went against the Committee of Public Safety during the Reign of Terror in France. He hated the sight of guillotines, and while stationed at the village of Saint-Maurice, he had one removed, broken, and burned. This act displeased the committee so much that they wanted to have Dumas guillotined. He was saved by his reputation and his influential friends. It also earned him the nickname of "Monsieur de l'humanité."[96] He was leading a quiet, retired life at Villers-Cotterets in 1797 when Napoleon launched his Egyptian campaign. Missing the military life, he accepted the challenge to go back into action. This would bring about his downfall.[97]

As the war continued, Napoleon's generals became anxious and suspicious of Napoleon's real intentions. Unlike the others, Dumas was not the type to hold his tongue. He believed in peace and a republican form of government. His view on this came to a head. It ended badly, and Dumas requested permission to return home.

On the way, he and those that left with him were caught in a storm at sea, and while sheltering in Tarentum, they were captured by the Bourbon government of Naples, a sworn enemy of France. Dumas and company were placed in prison and remained there for two years under very difficult conditions. By the time Dumas was released, Napoleon was first consul. With their friendship completely destroyed, Dumas was forced to retire and received no payment of indemnity for his ill treatment by the Neapolitan government. Dumas returned to Villers-Cotterets with a pension of only 160 pounds. Dumas had one daughter, Aimie Alexandrine Dumas, who was eight when her father returned. In 1802, a son was born who was to have his father's name. He would become one of France's greatest writers. Dumas's last years were not happy ones. He spent his last days trying to get money that was owed to him for his time in prison, but he was never successful. Alexandre Dumas died on February 26, 1806, at the age of forty-four from a fatal disease he caught while in prison.[98] His name can be found on the Arc de Triomphe.[99]

Le général Dumas au pont de Clausen

2. **Alexandre Dumas, Père** was of Haitian descent. He was born to General Alexandre Dumas and Marie Labouret on July 24, 1802 in Villers-Cotterets.[100] Dumas was one of the most successful writers in France's history. He helped start the romantic movement on the French stage. Dumas produced more works of literature than anyone in history. This collection consists of novels, memoirs, and books of travel, numbering over three hundred volumes, including twenty-five volumes on drama.

He also had several collaborations; the best known of these was with Maquet. His most famous works are: *The Three Musketeers*, *Georges*, *The Viscount of Bragelonne*, *The Forty-Five*, *The Black Tulip*, and *The Count of Monte Cristo*. Two of his works, *The Three Musketeers* and *The Count of Monte Cristo*, would have been enough to classify him as one of the best writers in history.[101]

Alexandre Dumas's father, it would seem, was a great source of adventure for his tales. Tom Reiss states the following:

> Alex's son, Alexandre Dumas, gave his father uncredited starring roles in some of the most famous swashbuckling adventures in all of literature.[102]

Resis continues:

> One account reported that he [the father] fought and won three duels in one day. (Reiss says that this was most certainly an inspiration for a scene in *The Three Musketeers* when d'Artagnan challenges the three musketeers to battle in one afternoon. The scene ends with the phrase, "All for one, and one for all.").[103]

He was like his father and was successful in being a soldier, duelist, hypnotist, cook, gourmet, entertainer, bon vivant, champion of human rights, and excavator of buried cities. Dumas was strongly against slavery and stated the following in a letter to the bishop of Autun, thanking him for his fight against it: "There may even be relatives of mine who even now are forming part of the cargoes of slave vessels."[104]

Dumas played a small role in the Revolution of 1840, but like his father before him, he also broke with the governing body for support of the French Republic, an act that forced him to flee to Switzerland. After squandering his money, he began writing to regain his fortune. However, his style of writing was no longer in fashion. Soon his health began to fail, and he was forced to live with his son and daughter. Alexandre Dumas, Père, died on December 5, 1870 in the arms of his son. [105] His talent was so great that Europe adored him, and Americans clamored for his novels. His dramas made Africa, where they were played in Egypt for Mehemet-Ali.

3. **Alexandre Dumas, File** was of Haitian descent. He was the last member of this great family that the world would come to know. Dumas was born on July 17, 1824 in Paris to Dumas, Père, and Marie Labay, a dressmaker.[106] He was a leading reformer of France, and his plays, poems, and essays were full of attacks on the evil practices of the time. His best and most famous work was the play *Camille* in 1848, which was written in the defense of a "fallen woman." It made Dumas one of the leading playwrights of this period. Other major works included *Le Fils Naturel, Le Père Prodigue, La Question d'Argent, Le Demi-Monde, Diane de Lys, La Princess Georges, Les Idées de Madame Aubray, L'Étrangère,* and *Francillon.* In each, he emphasized social and psychological problems. Although not as great a writer as his father, he himself stated that he received more respect and honor. Dumas became a member of the French Academy of Arts and Sciences in 1874, which had denied his father induction. He accepted his membership in the name of his father, who had already passed on. He also criticized them for the lack of respect they had shown his father.[107]

Alexandre Dumas died on November 27, 1895 at the age of seventy-one, having never visited Haiti, the birthplace of his ancestors.

In the Place Malsherbes, Paris, three statues stand: one for each of the Dumas men, three great men of Haitian heritage and descent.

The Lewis Family

Mary Edmonia Lewis was a Haitian American woman who was born in upstate New York to a Haitian father and Chippewa mother. Not only was she one of the leading sculptors of her day, but she was also the first African American artist to achieve international fame.[108] Reporters and newspapers described her as such.

A reporter in Rome, upon viewing her work, stated the following:

An interesting novelty has sprung up among us, in the city where all our surroundings are of the olden time. Miss Edmonia Lewis, a lady of color, has taken a studio here, and works as a sculptress in one of the rooms formerly occupied by the great master Canova. She is the only lady of her race in the United States who has thus applied herself to the study and practice of sculptural art.[109]

An American newspaper reported the following: "No men hold a position in the world of art equal to this colored artist."[110]

She was also a successful and shrewd businesswoman who had earned $100,000 in commissions by 1873. She received requests for various works, such as statues, headstones, and even altars. Famous and powerful individuals of her day, such as President Ulysses S. Grant and Pope Pius IX, visited her studio.[111]

Mary Edmonia Lewis

Samuel W. Lewis was born in Haiti and was the half brother of the great African American artist Mary Edmonia Lewis. When he was a child, his parents immigrated to America. After the death of his mother, his father married a Chippewa woman, who became the mother of his half sister, Edmonia. At the age of twelve, his father died, and he (Samuel) became a barber.[112] After traveling to Europe, Lewis returned to the United States to explore gold mining in California, Oregon, and Idaho, supporting himself by working as a barber.

He was also a successful entrepreneur, making his money though real-estate investments. Lewis moved to Bozeman, Montana, were he became one of its prominent citizens. In Bozeman, "he built the Lewis Block on the south side of East Main Street, which housed a number of businesses, including his barber shop and bath house."[113] Besides owning his own home, he also built and owned four rental homes, two of which still exist today on South Tracy.[114] In 1859, he encouraged his famous sister to apply to Oberlin College, one of the few colleges that accepted black women. He supported her studies at Oberlin and later sent her abroad to study art in Florence, where she became a noted sculptor.[115]

He had one son, Samuel E. Lewis, by his wife, Melissa Bruce, who was a widow with six children when she married Lewis. When he died on March 28, 1896 at the age sixty-three, one of the pallbearers at his funeral was the mayor of Bozeman, Frank L. Benepe, who also gave the eulogy. The *Avant-Courier* reported, "The funeral was largely attended, hundreds of our citizens going to the residence to pay their sincere respect to the memory of the very worthy old-time citizen, and a large number of our citizens in carriages joined the sad procession to the 'silent city of the dead.'"

His lengthy obituary in the *Avant-Courier* read "firm friend, an enterprising, public spirited citizen, a pleasant neighbor, a kind husband and affectionate father." His grave is marked with an obelisk monument.[116]

Property of Samuel W. Lewis

12

Haitian Fighting Style

1. **Guerrilla warfare.** Toussaint Louverture's army of disciplined ex-slaves taught conventionally trained military men the meaning of guerrilla warfare and ran circles around the British.[117]

2. **Stick-fighting and machete fencing.**

> Enslaved people utilized stick fighting in dances as well as violent duels over impugned honor throughout the Circum-Caribbean ... Behind this seemingly innocuous public dance, however, was the *juego de garrote*, a more clandestine martial art that utilized the stick, knife, and machete. Medéric Moreau de Saint-Méry, a member of the Superior Council of Saint Domingue in the 1780s, described the use of fighting sticks by the enslaved in duels that were preceded by a ritual challenge and oath.[118]

> [Among the blacks] differences are settled, [with] a fight with sticks ... The blacks handle this club with great skill and since they always aim for the head, the blows which they received are always serious. And so, the combatants are soon all blood.[119]

Distraught over the potential of such duels, he lamented that the "police have indeed forbidden these clubs and keep confiscating them, but they are so easily replaced that it does no good." Although he was clearly wary of the art's harmful potential, Moreau de Saint-Méry later described the art as a sport and admired the ability of its adepts:[120]

This fatal club serves also to make the negro's skill dazzling in one sort of combat. One cannot help admiring with what speed the blows are launched–and avoided–by two practiced men. They maneuver around each other to gain the advantage while holding the club and swinging it with both hands. Then, suddenly, a blow is directed, the other parries, and attack and riposte alternate, until one of the fighters is hit by the other. This normally ends the fight. The sport has its own rules, just as fencing does. A new athlete takes the place of the beaten one and the palm goes to the most adroit …[121]

These stick-fighting skills helped train bondsmen in the mastery of the machete as well.[122]

Even after the end of slavery, the masters of Haitian machete fighting continued to teach in a progression from training with sticks to the mastery of the machete. An aspirant in this system first learned *tiré bwa*, the art of fencing with sticks as a way to learn the strikes and defenses of the system in relative safety. Only after achieving some proficiency in tiré bwa did masters then teach the student *tiré coutou* (knife) or, more importantly, at least one of the many styles of *tiré machet,* the art of machete fighting. Although basic proficiency could be attained in less than half a year of training, mastery required much higher levels. The test of graduation of mastery often involved defending oneself blindfolded or in a complexly dark room. In order to pass this test, the student had to master a system called "the secret of Dessaline," which developed the skill of allowing a master to fight without the use of his eyesight.[123]

3. **YouTube Haitian Machete-Fencing Videos**. There are sixteen videos in total in this link: http://www.youtube.com/user/generalrelative#p/u.

4. *Muti, Stick/Blade/Knife Fighting Martial Art of Haiti* (minutes 3:54).

"A short film on the art of Muti. An art imported from the Kongo/ Angola region of Africa and spread to South America from Haiti." http://www.youtube.com/watch?v=-F5hbEX8V6w.

5. Haitian stick-fighting is also known as *kalenda, tiré baton, tire bwa,* and other names.[124]

6. **African martial traditions.** "In eigtheenth-century Saint-Domingue (Haiti), a mulatto called Jerome (a.k.a. Stake) sold *mayombo* (fighting sticks) that supposedly gave their users the power to defeat opposing stick fighters 'at no risk to themselves.'

"Additional details about Jerome's practices show that he was a practitioner of the religion called *vodun* (voodoo). This religion derived from the same West African sources (Kongo, Angola, Dahomey) as did Cuban *santería* and Brazilian c*andomblé.* Although contemporary Europeans labeled Jerome a witch and accused him of mesmerism, the ties to African martial traditions of supernaturally strengthening weapons are clear."[125]

7. **African Haitian martial arts.** *Pinge* was developed by the African slaves residing there for the same reasons as *machet'e* and *capoeira.*

8. **Yves Jabouin (**1979–) was born in Port-au-Prince, Haiti. He fights in Montreal. He is a mixed martial artist who currently competes in the bantamweight division of the UFC under the nickname "Tiger."

9. **Ovince St. Preux** (1983–) is a Haitian American born in Miami, Florida, of Haitian immigrants. He is a mixed martial-arts artist.

10. **Jean Phoenix Le Grand** (1965–) is Haitian martial artist in tae kwon do. He comes from a long line of martial artists. Both of his parents are black belts, and two of his uncles are grandmasters.

11. **David Loiseau** (1979–) is a Haitian Canadian mixed martial artist from Montreal, Quebec. His nickname is "The Crow."

Negres de St. Domingue se battabtau bâton

NÉGRES JOUANT AU BÂTON.

Negres Jouant au baton

13

Inventors

1. **Marc B. Auguste Sr.**, Haitian born, was "instrumental in the development and the prototyping of a multi-purpose portable coin-organizer. He shares intellectual property rights with his eldest son, Marc Auguste Jr. and his daughter-in-law, Jacqueline A. Johnson-Auguste."[126] It was invented to help individuals who are visually impaired. The device has proven to be popular and useful to the sighted population as well.[127] It is US Patent Number 7,083,512 and Canada Patent Number CA 2392678.

2. **Michel Frantz Molaire** (Mike F. Molaire). This Haitian-born chemist, inventor, photographer, poet, and publisher came to the United States at the age of twenty-one. He holds fifty-seven US patents and more than 120 international patents. Molaire holds an AAS chemical technology degree from New York Technical College, BS degree in chemistry, MS degree in chemical engineering/polymer science, and MBA management degree from the University of Rochester. He worked for Kodak for thirty-six years, leaving in 2010.[128] Mr. Molaire has received many awards and recognitions for his achievements in his field.[129]

Michel Frantz Molaire is also an author, and he has written a collection of poems in both French and English—*La Vie des Oiseaux Morts* (in French), *Plus Pres,* and his first English collection, *Shadow of Dreams.*[130]

3. **J. L. Pickering** of Gonaives, Haiti, West Indies, patented a dirigible-type airship (1899) three years before Orville and Wilbur Wright received intellectual property rights on their flying machine with a motor.[131]

4. **Charles Terres Weymann.** (See "Pilots" chapter.)

5. Another area Haitians are making their presence felt is in the field of technology. A student group made up of almost entirely Haitian immigrants, some of who emigrated from Haiti after the earthquake in 2010, won first place in a robot competition at the Javits Center. Their robot outperformed robots from sixty-three other schools around the country, including leading science high schools such as Stuyvesant and Dalton. For their accomplishment, their school was one of just two public school teams from New York invited to the FIRST (For Inspiration and Recognition of Science and Technology) Tech Challenge held in April in St. Louis, where they competed against one hundred schools from around the world to see who could build the fastest and most precise robot.[132]

14

Law and Politics

1. **Ertha Pascall-Trouillot** is a woman of many firsts. She was the first woman to serve as a civil court judge in the 1980s, became the first woman chief justice in 1988, and two years later, by unanimous consent of the council, she became the first woman president of Haiti.[133]

2. **Sonia Pierre** was a human rights activist who bravely fought discrimination against the poor Dominicans of Haitian descent. She was born one of twelve children in the Dominican Republic to Haitian immigrants. For her human rights activities, she received the Amnesty International award in 2003. In 2007, she was recognized for her work in securing citizenship and education for Dominican-born ethnic Haitians and honored with the Robert F. Kennedy Human Rights Award. Her fight for change started early at the age of just thirteen when she led her fellow Dominicans of Haitian descent on a march for cane cutters' rights. It led to her first arrest, and she was threatened with deportation. Ms. Pierre died on December 4, 2011 at the age of forty-eight of a heart attack. She is survived by three children.[134]

3. **Patrick Gaspard** was the director of the White House Office of Political Affairs and was the highest-ranking Haitian American official in the Obama administration.[135] Gaspard's political background includes the following:

- served as the executive vice president of Politics and Legislation for Local 1199 SEIU, United Healthcare Workers East, the largest local union in America
- worked for Jesse Jackson's presidential campaign in 1988
- served as political director for Bertha Lewis, who was the head of ACORN's New York chapter

- served as the director of President Barack Obama's Office of Political Affairs from January 2009 to January 2011
- became executive director of the Democratic National Committee in January 2001[136]

Gaspard was born in Kinshasa, Zaire. His family had fled there from the Duvalier dictatorship of Haiti. Later, the family immigrated to the United States.[137]

4. **Michaëlle Jean** is a Haitian who made Canadian history on September 27, 2005 by becoming the first person of African Caribbean heritage to hold the position of governor general of Canada. She was the third woman and the second immigrant to be assigned to this post.[138] Another first, Madame Jean was the first black person to declare the 2010 Vancouver Olympic Winter Games open. This is an honor reserved for the hosting country head of state.[139] At the end of her five-year post, Gov. Gen. Michaëlle Jean was given a twenty-one-gun salute during her final appearance before the Canadian forces as their commander in chief.[140] "On May 12, 2010, Princess Margriet of the Netherlands unveiled the Michaëlle Jean Tulip, a dark maroon tulip (a new cultivar of the "Triumph" class) honoring Canada's Governor General that will be registered with the Dutch Royal General Bulb Growers' Association."[141]

5. **Anne-Louise Mésadieu** was the first woman of Haitian descent elected to a council in France.

6. **Dr. Firmin Monestime** was born in Haiti, immigrated to Canada in the 1940s, and made history by becoming the first black mayor in a Canadian municipality. After taking a year off for health reasons, he again became mayor and remained so, often by acclamation, until his death. In 1975, he founded the Algonquin Nursing Home, a private and highly respected seniors' community in Mattawa. (His daughter, Vala Monestime Belter, continues to run the home.) In 1975, a provincial township was named in his honor for his outstanding

service to the province. Dr. Monestime studied and specialized in rural medicine and wrote three books on the subject.[142]

7. **Mathieu Eugene**, in 2007, became the first Haitian-born elected to office in the state of New York.

8. **Kwame Raoul** is the pride of Haitians in Illinois. In 2004, he became the first Haitian senator in the state of Illinois. He replaces Barack Obama as the first African American elected to the United States senate in the twenty-first century. He was born in Chicago, Illinois, on September 30, 1964, to Haitian-born immigrants, the late Janin Raoul, MD, and Marie Therese Raoul. He is a former Cook County prosecutor. Raoul earned his bachelor's degree in political science from DePaul University and a law degree from Chicago-Kent College of Law in 1993. He is married to Kali Evans-Raoul, who is a professional image consultant and admitted responsibility for shaping her husband's polished style. They have two children—a son, Che, and daughter, Mizan.[143]

9. **Michaelle Solages,** on November 6, 2012, became the first Haitian elected to the New York State Assembly.

10. **Noramie Festa Jasmin** made history on December 7, 2009 by becoming the first female mayor of the village of Spring Valley, New York, and the very first Haitian American mayor in New York State.

11. **Margareth Jourdan** is Haitian native who in 2001 became the first Haitian American judge in Spring Valley as well as the first black woman judge in Spring Valley.

12. Eleven percent of African American attorneys are of Haitian origin, according to a statement written to the US Senate Subcommittees of Foreign Relations on International Development and Foreign Assistance and Western Hemisphere.[144]

15

Medical

1. **Francois Fournier De Pescay** was born in France and was part Haitian. His father was François Pescay, a planter of Saint-Domingue, and his mother was a free black woman, Adélaïde Rappau. During his lifetime, he would become one of France's greatest physicians. He was a professor of pathology, regimental surgeon-major, chief surgeon of the Paris police, and chief health officer of France. De Pescay was also the private doctor of Ferdinand VII, the king of Spain. Louis XVIII in 1814 appointed him director of health and hygiene for the French army. In addition to compiling a medical dictionary, he also wrote a great deal on vaccination, tetanus, scrofula, and other maladies, and he was a biographer of note.[145]

2. **Dr. Rose-Marie Toussaint** is a Haitian-born surgeon. She is one of only two practicing female liver-transplant physicians in the United States. She graduated from Loyola University in New Orleans, Howard University Medical School, and interned and trained for three years at the renowned transplant center of the University of Pittsburgh Medical School. She specializes in both liver and kidney transplants.[146] She is the author of *Never Question the Miracle: A Surgeon's Story.*

3. **Dr. Rodrigue Mortel** was born of humble beginnings in Saint-Marc, Haiti; however, this did not stop Mortel from becoming the most respected and renowned Haitian scientist of the century. His "research findings were adopted as the protocol for standard treatment for uterine cancer in the United States."[147] Mortel was director of research at the Curie Institute and is now coordinator of the Cancer Center at Pennsylvania State University Medical Center.

Mortel has given back to his hometown of Saint-Marc by building a school for children in need.[148]

4. Ten percent of African American doctors are of Haitian origin, according to a statement written to the US Senate Subcommittees of Foreign Relations on International Development and Foreign Assistance and Western Hemisphere.[149]

16

Military, Revolts, Revolutions, and Wars

America

Revolution

1. Many people are unaware of the role Haitians played in the history of the United States and particularly of the city of Savannah, Georgia. It was there in 1779 that eight hundred free and enslaved black Haitians aided in the fight for American independence from British post-revolutionary threats. Three of these individuals later became famous in their own countries. Henri Christophe, who was fourteen years old at the time of his service, later became a famous general and king of Haiti. Martial Besse was promoted to general by the French. Jean-Baptiste Mars Belley was a leader of Haiti and deputy of the convention.[150] In Savannah at Franklin Square, there is a monument in honor of those who took part in this battle. The organization that led the charge for this monument is the Haitian American Historical Society (visit its website at http://haitianhistory.org/index.html).

2. **Chasseurs-Volontaires de Saint-Domingue** was a volunteer regiment made up of ten companies of light infantry (chasseurs) enlisted from "free men of color."

   - Haitians from all parts of St. Domingue volunteered to fight: "… volunteer legion had taken place not only in the two cities, Cap-François and Port-au-Prince, but in every province the length and breadth of the land. In Léogane, in Jérémie, in Tiburon, in St. Marc the volunteers came forward, registered in the parish church …"[151]

- Of their bravery, the following has been said: "The Chasseurs Volontaires de Saint Domingue covered themselves with glory during the retreat and reembarkment after having conducted themselves with courage during the all-out attack on Savannah. The black and mixed blood soldiers and officers of Saint-Domingue protected the retreat of American and French forces and permitted the embarkment of the French forces."[152]

- They were sold into slavery by the British: "In May 1780 over 60 Chasseurs were captured when Charleston, South Carolina fell to the British. The British Navy also captured three transports carrying Chasseurs. These soldiers were considered prizes of war and were sold into slavery."[153]

- The colonial Du Cap regiment of infantry from St. Domingue also fought in the siege of Pensacola: "A unit made up of Haitians took part in the successful allied (French and Spanish) campaign against British-held Pensacola in May 1780. Here the Haitians faced some of the same British regiments that their comrades had faced in Savannah."[154]

- They also were at Yorktown: "Throughout the war, French *américanophile* such as Pierre Augustin Caron de Beaumarchais used Saint-Domingue as a major transshipment center for weapons smuggled to U.S. rebels, while the French navy established an important base in Cap Français (the fleet that helped defeat the British squadron near Yorktown in 1781 had sailed from that port)."[155]

- St. Domingue traded with America: "When the United State became independent in 1783—the first colony to do so in the Western Hemisphere—it found itself rather isolated economically. Other colonies were bound by colonial trade rules that banned commerce with third-party countries; thus, U.S. merchants had nobody to trade with, except for St.

Domingue. France, unable to satisfy its colony's surging demand for food and timber, introduced some loopholes into its mercantilist regulations, and an active U.S.—Dominguian trade (part legal, part contraband) soon began. By the 1790s, St. Domingue was the United States second-largest trading partner after England."[156]

Sam Fraunces.

3. **Samuel Fraunces**, known as "Black Sam," was a soldier of the American Revolution and was the owner of the famous Fraunces's Tavern located on Pearl Street in New York City.[157] He was called Black Sam because "... of his tan complexion and his tight, curly hair. Keeping with the time, he often wore a white, powdered wig."[158] He was described as follows:

He was called Black Sam, but he was, and still is, described as being white, Negro, colored, Haitian, and mulatto.[159]

While researching the story of his life, it was discovered that Fraunces' racial identity was recorded as Negro, colored, Haitian Negro, Mulatto, 'fastidious old Negro' and swarthy.[160]

Fraunces arrived in New York City from the Caribbean in 1762 and opened his now-famous tavern. Before changing its name, it was known as "Sign of Queen Charlotte" and then "Sign of the Queen's Head," not receiving its present name until 1770. His establishment was well known even in his day for its great food and wines.[161] But today it is more famous for the historical events that took place there. It was the location where New York's Sons of Liberty met and planned their own Boston-style tea party and where George Washington made his famous farewell speech to his officers.[162] In his tavern, he established a course of lectures on national philosophy and opened an exhibition of seventy wax figures.[163]

When the British occupied the city, Fraunces signed up as a patriot soldier and fought with George Washington. He also became a spy, gave money, and housed and fed American soldiers and prisoners. Washington thanked Fraunces with these words after the war: "You have invariably through the most trying times maintained a constant friendship an attention to the cause of our country and its independence and freedom."[164] Congress sent him a letter citing both his generous support of American prisoners and his secret service during the war.[165]

When Washington became president, he asked Fraunces to serve as the first steward in his president's house in New York. Fraunces made sure that the presidential table was "bountiful and elegant." When the nation's capital relocated to Philadelphia in 1790, so did Fraunces.[166] After four years, on June 9, 1794, Fraunces left his position as steward and opened a restaurant called Tavern Keeper on 166 Second Street. The following year, he moved again and relocated the tavern, naming it the Golden Tun Tavern. It was located on South Water Street and was a place that Washington, along with other dignitaries, dined.[167] He introduced Washington to carrot cake, popularizing it as a dessert. "Washington's celebrated enslaved chef Hercules was taught much of his art by Fraunces and emulated his mentor right down to his affinity for fancy clothes. 'Hercules was important,' said Charles Blockson, emeritus curator of the Charles Blockson Afro-American Collection at Temple University and a founder of Generations Unlimited, 'but even the way he dressed he got from Fraunces.'"[168]

Samuel Fraunces died on October 12, 1792 at the age of seventy-two and was buried in an unmarked grave at St. Peter's Church in Philadelphia.[169] In recent years, his racial identity has become the subject of some debate. Stephan Salisbury proclaims in his article, "Many in the African American community dismiss scholarly claims that Fraunces was a white man. And at least some of his multihued descendants consider that assertion obtuse."[170] C. R. Cole, a Fraunces descendant by marriage, states, "The Fraunces family is African in origin," said Cole. "The family totally understands they are mixed racial. Everyone understands that." He goes on to say, "How could a family so intertwined with so many individuals associated with the Revolution (American) not be remembered?" Cole answered: "Because he's mulatto."[171] Also Charles Blockson—as far as he is "concerned, there is no question about the racial identity of the steward and tavern owner: Fraunces was a black man of Haitian descent."[172] On June 26, 2010, Samuel Fraunces was finally given the honors he deserved by having his name inscribed on an obelisk in the churchyard of St. Peter's in Philadelphia, where he is buried in an unmarked grave.[173]

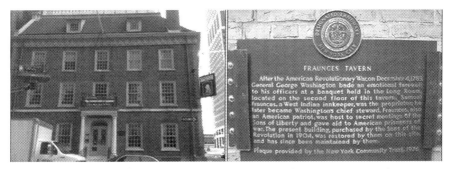

Fraunces Tavern at 54 Pearl Street, Manhattan, New York, along with commemorative plaque (photo by M. Charlot)

Leader of the Black Auxiliaries for King Carlos IV

BIASOU
Primer Gefe delos Negros de Sant Domingo

4. **Jorge Biassou**, whose real name was Georges Biassou, led an army of Black Auxiliaries for King Carlos IV.

General Jorge Biassou of St. Augustine is a name that belongs in the book of great names in world military history. He has not been forgotten by history; there are numerous websites that offer testimony of his life. He is included in a book by Jane Landers, *Black Society in Spanish*

Marjorie Charlot

Florida, and he was the basis of a character in the critically acclaimed novel, *All Souls Rising* by Madison Smartt Bell.

It is not common knowledge that Biassou was instrumental in Haiti becoming a free republic. In the last decade of the eighteenth century, Biassou was one of the leaders who instigated the Haitian slave uprising. He is credited with convincing Toussaint Louverture to make the fight against the French to gain freedom for the enslaved blacks of Haiti, his cause as well. Biassou and Louverture fought with the Spanish against the French. Biassou would be named a general by the Spanish. However, when the French promised to free the slaves, Toussaint allied with them against the Spanish. Biassou remained loyal to the Spanish and was defeated by Louverture.

In 1795, Biassou left Haiti and became a Spanish citizen, moving to Florida, which then was a colony of Cuba. Biassou even changed his name from Georges to Jorge. Wealthy and respected in the St. Augustine community, Biassou earned the second highest wages of any official in Florida and was given the command of the free black militia stationed at Fort Matanzas. His home on St. George Street in St. Augustine, Florida, which was known as Salcedo House, is now the headquarters of Whetstone's Chocolates. Biassou was eulogized at the cathedral by the Catholic Church and is interred at Tolomato Cemetery, where he rests alongside many of the pillars of St. Augustine's history. Though he lived a life of distinction, it is ironic that his grave marker makes no notation of his ever having attained the rank of general.

Battle of New Orleans—War of 1812

1. **Joseph Savary** was a native black Haitian who was a veteran of the Haitian Revolution and a former French republican officer. Savary was the first African American soldier to achieve the rank of second major under Andrew Jackson in New Orleans on December 19, 1814.[174]

64

2. **Haitian soldiers:**

As British forces threatened to invade New Orleans in 1814, American authorities sought to win the loyalty of battle-hardened black soldiers like Colonel Savary [native black Haitian who was a veteran of the Haitian Revolution and a former French republican officer]. They were also well aware of the prominent role that free men had played in slave rebellions. With the English approaching, pacifying them would be strategically sound.

General Andrew Jackson arrived in New Orleans in December 1814 and immediately mustered 350 native-born black veterans of the Spanish militia into the United States Army. Colonel Savary raised a second black unit of 250 of Haiti's refugee soldiers. Jackson recognized Savary's considerable influence and knew of his reputation as "a man of great courage." On Jackson's orders, Savary became the first African-American soldier to achieve the rank of second major.

The Haitians in Barataria also fought in the battle of New Orleans. In September 1814 federal troops invaded their community and dispersed the Lafittes and their followers. Hundreds of refugees poured into the city. Andrew Jackson offered them pardons in return for their support in defending the city. After the victory, he commended the two battalions of six hundred African-American and Haitian soldiers whose presence in a force of three thousand men had proved decisive. He praised the "privateers and gentlemen" of Barataria who "through their loyalty and courage, redeemed [their] pledge … to defend the country."

Jackson observed that Captain Savary "continued to merit the highest praise." In the last significant skirmish of the battle, Savary and a detachment of his men volunteered to clear the field of a detail of British sharpshooters. Though

Savary's force suffered heavy casualties, the mission was carried out successfully.

Within weeks of the victory, however, Jackson yielded to white pressure to remove the men from New Orleans to a remote site in the marshland east of the city to repair fortifications. Savary relayed a message to the general that his men "would always be willing to sacrifice their lives in defense of their country as had been demonstrated but preferred death to the performance of the work of laborers." Jackson, though not pleased, refrained from taking any action against the troops. In February, the general even lent his support to Savary's renewed efforts to rejoin republican insurgents in Mexico.[175]

Civil War

1. **Louis Noisette** was a second-generation Haitian American who fought for the Union Army, serving as a drummer boy in Savannah from May to June 1865. Pvt. Noisette was a member of the Thirty-Third Union Army's United States Colored Troops (USCT). After the war, he settled in Savannah. He died in 1891 and was buried in an unmarked gravesite in Laurel Grove Cemetery South.[176] In 2007, a marker was placed on Noisette's grave.[177]

2. **Captain Henry Louis Rey** was an Afro-Creole of Haitian heritage. He was born into a wealthy and prominent family from St. Domingue. He took part in the Civil War and Reconstruction. He was a leader in many diverse areas: "as captain in the Confederate Louisiana Native Guard and later in the Union Army; as a member of the Louisiana State House of Representatives; as a city assessor in New Orleans' Third District; as a director of *La Société Catholique pour l'instruction des orphelins dans l'indigence* and as a board member of the Orleans Parish School Board; and as secretary of both the Masonic Fraternite #29 and *La Société d'Economie de l'Aide et d'Assistance Mutuelle* (Economy Society)."[178] Rey was captain of

his company, the Economy Native Guards, which consisted of one hundred men.[179]

Revolts

1. **North America's first slave revolt:** According to several authors, the first successful slave revolt to occur in North America was in 1526 on the San Miguel settlement near Pee Dee River (or Pedee River) in South Carolina. This colony was started by the Spaniard Lucas Vasquez de Ayllon, who was among the first to bring Negroes to the present confines of the United States. He was accompanied by five hundred Spaniards and one hundred African slaves from Haiti. This doomed colony was named San Miguel de Gualdape and was founded in the summer of 1526.[180] Within a few months, half of the members of the Spanish population died from malaria. Included in this death total was Ayllon himself, who died on St. Luke's day, October 18 of that year.[181] Historian and political activist Herbert Aptheker states, "Internal dissension arose, and the Indians grew increasingly suspicious and hostile."[182] The black population also revolted, setting fires to buildings before fleeing; in November 1526, they went to live with the native Indian population.[183] African American professor and civil rights supporter R. R. Wright wrote, "Thus Hayti, the place where Negro slaves were first introduced into the New World, was strangely enough the first to manifest an awful retribution against human slavery."[184] The 150 remaining Spaniards fled back to Haiti, leaving the blacks, after the Indians, as the first permanent inhabitants of what was to be the United States. Blacks found their own settlement in present-day eastern United States.[185] While Dr. Claud Anderson and Brant Anderson in their text, *More Dirty Little Secrets About Black History Its Heroes, and Other Troublemakers* Volume II, write that some of these blacks would stay along Pee Dee River while others went to Florida, which at the time was Spanish territory; they would build their own maroon colonies to avoid European whites, who started to arrive in North America in the 1600s.[186] Some of these blacks may have moved to Virginia, for these

two authors contend, "In part, this explains the presence of 32 Blacks in Jamestown, Virginia, population records though only 20 Black slaves had supposedly arrived in 1619 onboard a Dutch slave ship."[187] Wright stated that "A singular incident connected with Ayllon's expedition along this coast is the fact that he, with the assistance of his Negro slaves, built the first ships constructed on our coast."[188] This event took place ninety-four years before the *Mayflower*.[189] Both authors proclaim, "Over two centuries after the Pee Dee River revolt, Stephen Foster wrote a song about the Pee Dee River and enslaved Blacks. His brother thought Foster should pick another river for the name of his song. After looking through an atlas, the brother came upon the Suwannee River in Florida and convinced Foster to change the song's title to 'Suwannee River.' Thus, few Blacks have longed for their home on the 'Old Pee Dee River.'"[190]

The French Revolution

1. **Napoleon** had at last twelve Negro West Indian generals who served in France. These generals were General Alexander Dumas (Haitian), who was once Napoleon's superior officer,[191] André Rigaud (Haitian), Martial Besse (Haitian), B. Leveille, Antoine Clouatte, J. B. Belley (Haitian), Magloire Pelage, Alexander Pétion (Haitian), A. Chanlatte, Barthelmy, Villate, and Etienne V. Mentor.[192]

JEAN-LOUIS

2. **Jean Louis Michel** was a Haitian and one of the greatest swordsmen and duelists in history. Having no family, at the age of eight or nine he somehow got to France. During the French Revolution, very young boys trained in the army; one of these boys was Jean Louis. He stood with the rest of the company ready for inspection. The year was 1796, and he was eleven years old. A French colonel of a regiment got angry, not because of the color of his skin but rather

due to the fact that Louis was too small for a boy his age. However, he was given a chance thanks to a captain who pleaded for him. Louis was questioned by the colonel: "I suppose you brought with you your heathen voodoo practices from the West Indies?" It would seem that voodoo stereotyping of individuals from the Caribbean, especially Haitians, was done even then. His reply was, "No, monsieur, I read my Bible every day," indicating that he was a Protestant. At first he, was weak when it came to training, but his spirit and quick recovery from fatigue impressed his trainer, D'Erape. Within a week of his training, with the help of nourishing food, he began to show the signs of the great swordsman he was about to become. D'Erape took Louis under his private care and stated, "Someday, that boy is going to astonish the world."[193]

At seventeen, Louis showed no sign of his once-small physique; he was now tall and strong. He was also the first swordsman of the garrison, and for the next ten years, he served in active duty. He fought in Italy, Russia, Prussia, and Austria. By 1814, Louis was in the Thirty-Second Regiment in the Third Division and was a master of arms in his regiment, which was stationed in Madrid.[194] This division included an Italian regiment whose membered were recruited by Napoleon in Italy. To say that there was any animosity existing between the Italians and the French would be an understatement. To put a stop to all the fighting after a brawl in which one hundred men took part, leaving several dead, a general decided to let them fight it out.[195] He sent for the master of arms from the Italian regiment, Giacomo Ferrari of Florence, Italy's most famous swordsman, and asked him to pick fifteen of his best men. The same was done for Louis. The day of this event, the garrison of ten thousand men came to the parade grounds to witness what was about to happen while Ferrari came along with his best men. Louis, however, came alone. Jean Louis had named himself fifteen times, confident that he could take them all on; he was right. He fought Ferrari first, killing him, taking a two-minute rest before going back and taking on another opponent. He killed all of them in what seemed to be the same way as Ferrari—by piercing the heart. All were dead except two. Seeing that things had gone too far and fearing for Jean Louis's safety, a colonel asked him to stop. It took Jean Louis all of forty minutes to finish off thirteen opponents.[196]

Louis always tried to spare his opponents' lives, saying that "fencing is the art of conciliation." He retired from the army in 1830 and settled in Montpellier. While there, he started one of the most famous fencing schools of the time and developed his own style, which was taught in the French army as well as in most other fencing schools. To honor him, several schools in France bear his name, and tournaments were held for him, one of which was at Metz in 1850. Even the nobility took lessons from him. Louis even umpired the famous bout between Count de Bondy and Lafaugère. He was by this time very wealthy and a leading social figure. He and his wife, a French woman named Mlle. Veillard, had a daughter, who like her father was skilled with a sword and at one time dressed as a man, fought, and won a fight with a leading fencer. By the time of the death of his beloved wife in 1865, he was already blind in both eyes from cataracts, and by November 19 of the same year, he too died at the age of eighty. His descendants still live in Montpellier, France.[197]

Haiti

The Haitian revolutionary Creole prayer: "Good God, who makest the sun to light us from on high, who raisest up the sea and makes the storms to thunder—Good God, who watches over all, hidden in a cloud, protect us and save us from what the white men do to us … Good God, give us vengeance, guide our arms, give us help. Good God, grant us that freedom which speaks to all men!"[198]

Did you know that Haitians fought with three countries before they earned their freedom? They fought against the armies of the French, the English, and the Spanish.

Slavery and Slave Revolts

1. The end of the Haitian Revolution marked not only the first successful slave rebellion in Haiti but also the "only slave uprising in history to end with the foundation of a new country." The success of Haitians in their quest for freedom resulted in revolts throughout the Caribbean and America.[199]

2. **Padrejean** was the African slave of a Spaniard in Santo Domingo whom he had assassinated, and he took refuge at Tortoise. Padrejean led the first slave revolt in St. Domingue. This event took place in Port-de-Paix against the French colonists and their governor. In October 1679, twenty-five black slaves set out on a mission to cut the throats of all whites. Later they went to Margot Port, Le Borgne, and St.-Louis-du-Nord.[200] Buccaneers were hired to storm Padrejean's mountain stronghold inland of St. Louis. Many of the French in St. Domingue lost their lives before he was caught and killed along with other black maroons.[201]

3. It was the goal of Toussaint Louverture to go to Dahomey, West Africa, and use it as base to fight the slave trade. To achieve this, he raised six million gold francs. He entrusted this money to Stephen Girard, an American ship captain and a Frenchman by birth. After the capture of Toussaint, Girard kept the money, refusing to return it to Toussaint's family. Girard later became the richest American of his day.[202] It is Gragon-LaCoste in his *Life of Toussaint L'Overture* who names the sum of six million francs and says, "Girard, to give him his true name, never returned the million entrusted to his care following the events which deprived Toussaint of his liberty." He also wrote of the litigation that followed in the courts for the money left by Girard to the city of Philadelphia.[203] After his death in 1831, Girard left millions for the founding of Girard College in Philadelphia. He also requested that this college be for whites only. Money was also given to buy coal for the poor of Philadelphia; this again was to be for whites only.[204]

4. It was the slave rebellion on this island that helped put a stop to France's goal of building an empire in the New World, a rebellion that led France to sell its Louisiana Territory to the United States in 1803. Carved from this enormous territory are parts or all of the following twelve states: Louisiana, Texas, Arkansas, Missouri, Kansas, Iowa, Nebraska, North and South Dakota, Oklahoma, Minnesota, and Montana. If it were not for the Haitian rebellion, citizens of these states would possibly be speaking French instead of English.[205]

5. **General Donatien de Rochambeau, the Caligula of Haiti.** After French army General Charles Victor Emmanuel Leclerc died in November 1802, he was replaced by French General Donatien de Rochambeau. Leclerc had suggested his successor to Napoleon, describing him thus: "He is a person of integrity, a good military man, and he hates the blacks."[206] To say Rochambeau hated blacks would be an understatement, but he hated mulattoes even more, and he began a campaign of their extermination.

At Port-Républicain, he gave a great ball in which he invited several mulatto women. It was a great party, and at midnight, Rochambeau stopped the dancing and begged them to enter into the next apartment. It was lit with one lamp. Black draperies hung, in which white material figures as skulls were visible; in the four corners were coffins. The women, silenced and terrified, began to hear funeral chants sung by invisible singers, at which time Rochambeau informed them, "You have just assisted at the funeral ceremonies of your husbands and your brothers." The French shot and drowned mulattoes hundreds at a time. As for the wealthy ones, after killing them, they took their property, according to James.[207] Rochambeau may have been the first person in history to use what we today would call a gas chamber, for he had blacks and mulatto prisoners placed into the hold of a ship named *The Stifler* and then had sulfur burned throughout the night. In the morning, the bodies were dumped overboard to make room for more.[208] Haitian author A. J. Victor quotes French Commander Ratapel, who wrote to a friend, "France will never possess this country. In the past month we have drowned 4,000 [indigenous]."[209] The extermination of blacks was first suggested by Leclerc, who on October 16, 1802, wrote to Napoleon stating the following: "Here is my opinion about this country. We must destroy all the Negroes of the mountains, men and women. Keep only children under twelve years of age. Destroy half of the Negroes in the plains and not leave in the colony a single Negro who had worn a uniform. Otherwise the colony will never be at peace."[210] Rochambeau drowned so many people in the Bay of Le Cap that people in the district would not eat fish.[211] He most likely was following Napoleon's orders (he had taken Leclerc's advice) of genocide, for Napoleon had ordered the extermination of all Haitian blacks over the age of twelve.[212] While murder was being committed around him, Rochambeau threw great parties, stole, and abandoned himself to all kinds of pleasures with his numerous concubines. Victor proclaims that Rochambeau is known for two barbaric acts: the funeral party described previously and the use of dogs against blacks.[213]

The French created for themselves a form of entertainment similar to that of ancient Rome. Author Martin Ros records that this was done by the Caligula of St. Domingue, Rochambeau, who had hundreds of dogs* brought from Cuba to St. Domingue. Upon arriving on the island, these dogs were cheered by white women who, according to reports, even licked the foam that dripped from their muzzles.[214] Rochambeau insisted that these dogs be fed only "Negro meat." Often this "meat" was the flesh of black women and children.[215] These victims may have been the women and children taking shelter in the woods or caves during battles. French soldiers tracked them down, killed them, and fed their dead bodies to the dogs that accompanied

---

*   These dogs were bloodhounds that were trained to hunt people. Ros writes, "Kept in cages from the day they were born, they were continuously starved— and then let loose on dummies the size of people that were filled with blood and the intestines of animals. Thus trained, they were marked by small Spanish crosses that they wore around their necks." (Martin Ros in *Night of Fire the Black Napoleon and the Battle for Haiti,* page 194.) These dogs were also used against Jamaican maroons to help stop their revolts.

them. If there is any doubt as to what Rochambeau meant by "Negro meat," the following letter in Victor's text *In the Name of Liberty, A History of Haiti (Pre-1492–1806)* written by Rochambeau to a Sergeant-Major Romel quickly removes all doubts:[216]

15 Germinal Year 1
(April 5, 1803)

I send you, my dear commander, a detachment of 150 men of the National Guard of Le-Cap. It is accompanied by twenty-eight bulldogs. These reinforcements will enable you to complete your operations. I will not let you ignore that you will be provided with neither ration nor allowance to feed these dogs. You must feed them with niggers.

Affectionately
Donatien Rochambeau[217]

An arena was built in the courtyard of the old Jesuit monastery so that spectators could watch as dogs tore slaves to pieces. It was reported that one slave was driven into the arena and was not only bitten by the dogs but was also torn apart by them because they were full. General Jacques Boyer, called "le cruel," who may have been an avid spectator, solved this problem by rushing into the arena, slashing opened the abdomen of his "faithful servant," and pulling out the guts. At this point, the dogs attacked. While the dogs ate their victim, the crowd applauded and cheered while military music played. Whites who attended were disappointed that victims seemed to suffer so little pain. For blacks to have held up so well through their torments, they had to be possessed by the devil.[218] In March 1803, the very dogs Rochambeau sent to be used against blacks turned on the French. When Rochambeau learned of the progress of the insurrection of the south and the west, he moved the seat of the government to Port-au-Prince. It was also there that he had come up with the funeral-party idea.[219] By the end of the month, black and mulatto volunteers of Petit-Goâve, led by Lamarre, decimated Rochambeau's Honor Guard. The dogs sent, as Dubois states, proved sometime to be a liability to their master. He continued to write, "Ignorant of color prejudice," they attacked those who were fleeing, who "in this circumstance happened to be white." Many of the dogs ended up "eaten by starving French soldiers."[220]

Rochambeau's actions united blacks and mulattoes in their war against whites.[221] During this time, Haiti had a new rebel leader, Jean-Jacques Dessalines, who was voted leader after the death of General Toussaint Louverture.[222] In Dessalines, Rochambeau met his match, for he confronted Rochambeau blow for blow. James writes that the French killed five hundred blacks at Le Cap and buried them in a large hole dug while they waited for execution. Dessalines raised gibbets of branches and hanged five hundred [whites] for Rochambeau and other whites in Le Cap to see.[223] Lerone Bennett, Jr., an African American scholar, states, "If LeClerc and his successor, Rochambeau, wanted to play with fire, Jean-Jacques Dessalines was their man."[224]

War for war, crime for crime, atrocity for atrocity.
–Jean-Jacques Dessalines, liberator of Haiti

Left: bloodhounds attacking a black family in the woods. Right: the mode of training bloodhounds in St. Domingo and of exercising them, by Chafseur

6. **The gassing of Haitians by the French using sulfur.** Claude Ribbe, a respected historian and the author of the book *The Crimes of Napoleon (Le Crime de Napoleon)*, explains how Napoleon was the forerunner to Adolf Hitler and was actually the first madman to plot and methodically outline the systematic massacre of an entire population of people. Ribbe details how Napoleon, who was considered a soldier's soldier, respected neither the rules of war nor the laws of humanity. Between 1800 and 1804, Napoleon and his henchmen showed no mercy to the Haitians soldiers and citizens who they captured as part of the campaign to end the slave revolts and hold on to colony of Haiti. Haiti was an incredible source of wealth to the empire, as it was the largest producer of the world's coffee and sugar. Let us not forget that Haiti notoriously worked its slave population to death or killed them outright if they were considered troublesome. There was little to no respect for black flesh on this island. Napoleon's brother-in-law, General Charles Le Clerc, who he appointed counsel to Haiti, gave orders to shoot any Haitian male over twelve years of age. One of Haiti's own natural resources was extracted and employed as a method of mass destruction against her citizens. The sulphur dioxide that was used to suffocate more than one hundred thousand black Haitians on the French prison ships came from the volcanoes that ring the island nation. These prison ships, known as *etouffiers*, or "chokers," were designed to asphyxiate the prisoners slowly and painfully.

This military campaign and the use of gas chambers was documented by Antoine Metral, a historian who chronicled France's foray into Haiti and Napoleon's genocidal exploits in his seminal book, published in 1825, *Histoire de l'expedition des Francais a Saint-Domingue: Sous le consulat de Napoleon Bonaparte, 1802–1803.*

Metral's account reads with the matter-of-fact tone belying the cruel and inhumane tactics of execution the French used to kill other human beings. Metral states, "We varied the methods of execution, … at times, we pulled heads off; sometimes a ball and chain was put at the feet to allow drowning; sometimes they were gassed in the ships by sulphur."

It would appear that women also fought against and died at the hands of the French invaders. In another account of this mass slaughter by a historian, it is recounted, "We invented another type of ship where victims of both sexes were piled up, one against the other, suffocated by sulphur."[225]

Metral describes the dead as innumerable; black bodies were heaped up everywhere, left near the graveyards of churches for disposal. Later, when the body count became untenable, Metral described how they waited until nightfall to dispose of the remains and bodies of the thousands of people they murdered during the day. "When the cover of night was used to hide these outrages, those walking along the river could hear the noisy monotone of dead bodies being dropped into the sea."

To be fair, there were officers in the French navy who were outraged at the atrocities they were commanded to commit. Some even stated that they would have preferred a court martial rather than to live with the guilt of this lapse in their compassion for their fellow human beings. Despite the outcry from his own officers, Napoleon's plan was considered the method to get rid of the enemy most economically. The murderous plan was altered with the ships picking up prisoners and taking them out to sea to be killed and disposed. However, the bodies washed ashore or were dragged back to land, tangled in ships' hulls.[226]

The mode of exterminating the Black Army, as practiced by the French

7. Because slaves lacked weapons, Laurent Dubois, a professor of romance studies and history in *Avengers of the New World: The Story of the Haitian Revolution,* says that slaves used "startling ruse and ingenuity. They camouflaged traps, fabricated poisoned arrows, feigned cease-fires to lure the enemy into ambush, disguised tree-trunks as cannons, and threw obstructions of one kind or another into the roads to hamper advancing troops."[227] Slaves even came up with what can only be called an unusual version of a bulletproof vest. Dubois writes that it was noticeable when the rebels were advancing on Le Cap that they stood up to three volleys of shots. This was because they were "wearing a kind of light mattress stuffed with cotton as a vest to prevent the bullets from penetrating."[228] Some sacrificed themselves for freedom in ways that can only be called

courage; for example, they "suffocated the cannon of the enemy with their arms and bodies, and so routed them." They captured the cannon from their enemies even though they did not know how to use it, but they quickly learned.[229] Dubois stated, "One group took control of a battery along the coast, when a French ship fired on the battery to dislodge them; they braved a barrage of 250 cannon shots. They then used the cannon balls that had landed around them to fire back at the ship, which was seriously damaged before its crew managed to sail it away."[230]

8. Did you know that Toussaint's army of disciplined ex-slaves taught conventionally trained military men the meaning of guerrilla warfare and ran circles around the British,[231] centuries before Algeria, Vietnam, and Iraq? During England's five-year campaign to take control of St. Domingue, it lost over 60 percent of the twenty thousand men it sent. Journalist Hochschild wrote the following:

> British myth-making has long skillfully turned military withdrawals or defeats into noble moments of heroism: consider, in later times, the charge of the Light Brigade or Dunkirk. But the five-year campaign of St. Domingue was an exception. The colony's name has never appeared on a single British regimental banner. For the British, their failed attempt to take St. Domingue was a startling lesson in the difficulties of trying to impose one's will in a hot, violent, distant and ill-understood part of the world, not unlike the lessons the United States would learn in later times.[232]

The loss the British faced in St. Domingue was one of the greatest disasters in British imperial history.[233] Dessalines, the Tiger of Haiti, was also instrumental in aiding Toussaint in keeping both the British and Spanish forces at bay.[234]

9. **Dessalines at the Battle of Crête-à-Pierrot (Kreyòl: *Lakrèt-a-Pyewo*):**

The first [French] division which came up to the attack of Crête-à-Pierrot was that of Debelle. As soon as the French troops were seen in the redoubt, Dessalines opened the gates. *"The gates have been opened,"* he said, *"for those who do not feel themselves courageous enough to die; while there is yet time, let the friends of the French depart; they have nothing but death to look for here."* After having sent away all whom sickness or fear made desirous of going, he spread a train of gunpowder as far as the first gate, and, seizing a torch, exclaimed, *"Now for the first fire, I will blow up the fort, if you do not defend it."* During these things, the French were advancing, preceded by a herald (4th March, 1802). The herald held a letter in his hand. Dessalines ordered his men to fire. The herald fell dead. Firing began on both sides in real earnest. For several hours, it continued without an interval. The French rushed forward with their usual bravery and enthusiasm, but it was only to meet death. The moment they were within reach, the batteries were opened and the ground was strewed with dead. The General-in-chief, Debelle, was grievously wounded, as well as Brigadier-General Devaux. The division was compelled to fall back with the loss of four hundred men.[235]

10. During the Haitian Revolution, the French quickly learned of the caliber of the blacks in Haiti. Afro-Trinidadian historian C. L. R. James recorded many acts of bravery in his text. For example, three men were condemned to die by fire after being caught setting fire to a plantation. While two were on fire crying out in pain, the third, a nineteen-year-old bound in a way that he could not see the other two, called to them in Kréyòl, "You do not know how to die. See how to die." Twisting his bound body, he sat down and placed his feet on the flames and let them burn without making a sound. James writes of other acts of courage in the face of death. One man was given to the dogs to be eaten and did not give the enemy the satisfaction of letting them see him angry or weak. He stroked the

dogs and encouraged them while he presented them his limbs. James also records the bravery of women, many of whom were equally as brave as men. One such woman went to her death bravely and put her husband, Chevalier, a black chief, to shame. While he hesitated at the sight of the scaffold, she showed him how to die. She stated, "You do not know how sweet it is to die for liberty!" She would not allow her executioners to hang her. She took the rope and did it herself. Her words to her daughters who were also hanged along with her were, "Be glad you will not be the mothers of slaves."[236] A French general in the expeditionary army, Lemmonier-Delafosse, who witnessed this act of bravery, was shocked and wrote, "These are the men we have to fight!" Leclerc wrote about them, "These men die with incredible fanaticism; they laugh at death, and the same is true of the women."[237]

11. **Women fighters.** Women could also be found among maroon groups, and some even fought next to the men in 1758. "Women joined ranks with thirteen men, several armed with pistols, billhooks, and machetes, in an attack against Thomas Bouchet."[238]

Female fighters of the Haitian Revolution were often considered just "as courageous as and even more ferocious than the men."[239] Women in St. Domingue, like their men, also had a strong desire for freedom as well as vengeance. Women resisted slavery in their own way. Some of their methods were suicide, arson, poisoning, and large gatherings of slaves.[240] Lecturer Catherine Reinhardt claims that women "were far more troublesome than men and their insubordination frustrated the masters." She continues by stating, "Women engaged more frequently in verbal or physical confrontations with whites."[241]

During the war for freedom, they contributed in many ways. For example, they transported weapons for Antoine Métral, a writer who described how, under the bayonets of General Leclerc, slave women transported weapons by leaping from rock to rock until they disappeared into the woods.[242] Métral also stated the following:

The weaker sex became the stronger. Young women without voicing a single complaint either in the streets or at the public squares went valiantly before the scaffold. By their moving examples, they encouraged those who were hesitant in dying for liberty. Some were seen to display a surprising character trait by smiling in the face of death in the presence of their masters whose desire for vengeance was thereby thwarted.[243]

Women proved their bravery not only during slavery but throughout the war, and they faced death like true warriors. In one battle in the south, they made up the first wave of an attack, carrying bundles of brush meant to help the troops behind them cross trenches around a fortification, and were massacred by French musket fire, this according to Dubois.[244] Assistant professor at Virginia Commonwealth University, Bernard Moitt, also documents their story. "In Saint-Domingue, slave women may also have targeted the military. The National Guard, which camped on the Galiffet Plantation in the northern part of the island during the early years of the war of liberation, experienced high mortality." Métral stated, "Soldiers died in droves after repeatedly drinking water from a well into which the slaves had dumped copper utensils. Whether the slaves knew that copper in the water supply would become toxic is uncertain. Indeed, the water could have been contaminated before by other agents. However, the act of dumping appears to have been deliberate and would likely have been the work of slave women."[245] Moitt continued to state, "Women formed part of the rebel stronghold located in the heights of the Cahos Mountains, close to the shores of the Artibonite River, where the slave leaders, Toussaint-Louverture and Jean Jacques Dessalines, stored their weapons and spoils and planned and executed their fighting strategies."[246]

As one can see, these women were brave and determined to earn their freedom just like the men. The following is a list of just a few of the thousands of heroines who fought for freedom in Saint Domingue:

- **Marie-Jeanne Lamartinierre** fought at La Crête-à-Pierrot in the northwest part of Haiti with the other slaves.[247] She is considered by many as Haiti's version of Joan of Arc. For her defense of La Crête-à-Pierrot, she has "has become part of the national legend and has led to her adoption as 'le symbole de la femme soldat' [the symbol of the female soldier]," writes Boisvert.[248]

- **Sanite Belair** was authoritative, brave, and bold. She often accompanied her husband during his war activities and was a significant influence in his decision making.[249]

- **Victoria "Toya" Montou** fought against the French in the Cahos Mountains of the Artibonite region.[250]

- **Henriette Saint-Marc** obtained gunpowder and ammunitions for the insurgents during the revolution.[251]

- **Marie-Claire Heureuse** (also **Marie-Claire Heureuse Dessalines**) As A. J. Victor states *In the Name of Liberty, A History of Haiti (Pre-1492–1806)*, "All her life, she had remained faithful to the most sacred purpose of the Revolution: the well-being of Haiti's children."[252] She was the wife of Jean-Jacques Dessalines.

- **Améthyste (Princess)** was a mulatto who is known to history as Princess Améthyste. She was the leader of a company of Amazons in Haiti [Haiti]. She had become part of a *Ghioux* or Voodoo [*Voodoux*], a cult that was a sort of religious and dancing masonry, which was brought to St. Domingue by Arada Negroes.[253] Améthyste also influenced many of her followers to enter this cult. Some, if not all, of these women were part of Communauté des Religieuses Filles de Notre Dame du Cap-Français, an educational order for young girls. Améthyste was one of its brightest students. Author Carolyn E. Fick writes that, "They leave the convent at night to participate in ritual dances to the African chant, the words of which, inexplicable to the whites, were … an invocation to the rainbow serpent Mbumba, for protection against the evil powers of the 'white man,' the 'slave traders,' and 'the witches.' The schoolmistresses noticed a certain agitation among the Negresses that increased particularly after they sang this round, adopted to the exclusion of all others:"[254]

Eh! eh! Bomba eh! eh!	[Eh! eh! Rainbow spirit, eh! eh!
Canga bafio té	Tie up the BaFioti
Canga mousse [sic] délé	Tie up the whites
Canga do ki la	Tie up the witches
Canga li'	Tie them][255]

They also had adopted a uniform type dress, wrapping sashes of a predominantly red color around the body and wearing sandals on their feet. The night of the revolt, the sisters from the windows of their monastery, which overlooked the countryside and the city, could see the shadows of bare-breasted Negresses who belonged to the sect dancing to the mournful sound of the long, narrow tambourines and conch shells, and alternating with the moaning of the sacrificed creatures, claims Fick.[256] Améthyste, before the revolt of 1791, would be heard invoking the "En! eh! Mbumba" along with her companions at night.[257]

- **Catherine Flon** is the Betsy Ross of Haiti. Her picture was featured on a ten-gourdes Haitian banknote issued in 2000. She is the lady in purple sitting on the chair, with needle and thread in hand. She was waiting to join the blue piece to make the Haitian flag. The goddaughter of Jean-Jacque Dessalines, she played a huge role in the Haitian Revolution as a nurse. However, she is not remembered as a nurse but rather as the seamstress who sewed the first Haitian flag on the last day of the Congress of Arcahaie, on May 18, 1803. She was remembered as a symbol of unity.[258] May 18 is Haitian Flag Day.

Sanite Belair

12. **Three countries against one**. America's first president, George Washington, a slave owner, sided with the French slave owners. Upon hearing their pleas for help, Washington authorized then security of state Thomas Jefferson (also a slave owner) to send the French slave owners $40,000 in emergency relief as well as one thousand weapons. As repayment for funds loaned to American revolutionaries during the Revolutionary War, France requested $400,000 in emergency assistance be given to the slave owners of St. Domingue. Even Venezuela gave $400,000 in aid to Napoleon's fruitless bid to recapture Haiti.

13. There were many heroes that emerged at the end of the revolutionary war due to their acts of bravery. François Capois (1766 in Por-De-Paix, Oct 19, 1806 at Limonade) took part in the famous battle at La Cap, a battle that would prove to be the turning point of the war. After soundly defeating three of the very best of Europe's armies, those they had made slaves were now victors.[259] "Capois is also known as Capois-La-Mort (Capois "the Death"), a sobriquet he earned on the battlefield for dealing out death to many of his enemies. He fought at the Battle of Vertières. On Nov 18, 1803, Capois and his troops, the Haitian Ninth Brigade, had to cross a bridge that was dominated by the fort at Vertières. On horseback, he and his men

were met by heavy firing from the enemy but continued to advance.[260] Many would die, but they would close ranks and clamber past the dead, singing:[261]

In Haïtien Kréyòl

Grenadiers a l'assaut!
sa ki mouri zafe a yo.
Nan pwen mamam.
Nan pwen papa.
sa ki mouri, zafe a yo!
Grenadiers A l'assaut!

English Translation

Soldiers, attack!
Those who are dead do not matter.
In war there is no mother.
In war there is no father.
Those who are dead do not matter.
Soldiers, attack!

Capois had several bullets pass through his cap; one bullet hit his horse while another passed through his cap. Not letting this stop him, he got up, drew his sword, brandished it over his head, and ran onward, shouting, "En avant! En avant! (Forward! Forward!)." This act of bravery was witnessed by Rochambeau, who was watching from the rampart of Vertières, and Rochambeau guards were so impressed with Capoix's courage that they applauded him. During the middle of the charge, French drums rolled a sudden cease-fire to cease the battle.[262] A French hussar mounted his horse, rode toward Capoix, and shouted, "General Rochambeau sends compliments to the general who has just covered himself with such glory!" Then he saluted the Haitian warriors, returned to his position, and the fight resumed.[263] Frenchman Lemonier-Delafosse, who avidly supported

Haitian slavery a half century after the revolution, wrote the following on the black revolutionaries in his memoirs:

> But what men these blacks are! How they fight and how they die! One has to make war against them to know their reckless courage in braving danger … I have seen a solid column, torn by grape-shot from four pieces of cannon, advance without making a retrograde step. The more they fell, the greater seemed to be the courage of the rest.[264]

14. General Alexander Dumas had been asked but "… refused to command the expedition France sent against Louverture, who ended his days in a Napoleonic jail."[265]

15. After the revolution, the ex-slaves of Haiti created the first black empire outside Africa when they crowned Jean-Jacques Dessalines emperor of Haiti, and his wife, Marie-Claire Heureuse Félicité, became empress. It was after the assassination of Dessalines that Haiti created the first black republic. In fact, did you know Haiti had two emperors and one king?

- Haiti's first emperor was **Jean-Jacques Dessalines** (born c. 1758, West Africa—died Oct. 17, 1806, Pont Rouge, near Port-au-Prince, Haiti), who became Jacques I after the revolution of 1804.
- The second emperor was **Faustin Soulouque** (born 1782?, Petit-Goâve, Haiti—died Aug. 6, 1867), who declared himself Emperor Faustin I in 1849.
- The one king of Haiti was **Henri Christophe** (born Oct. 6, 1767, Grenada?—died Oct. 8, 1820, Milot, Haiti), who proclaimed himself King Henri I.

16. In January 1804, Dessalines, after officially declaring St. Domingue an independent nation, renamed it Haiti after the indigenous Arawak name meaning "the land of the mountains."

Emperor Jacques I

King Henri I

Emperor Faustin I

Battle at St. Domingue

Combat et prise de la Crête-à-Pierrot (Fight
and capture of Crête-à-Pierrot)

Top: Toussaint L'Ouverture, Jean Jacque Dessalines, and François
(Capois-LaMort.) Capois
Bottom: Alexande Sabes Petion and Henri Christophe

Adjutant General E. V. Menter. Served under Dessalines

General Jean Pierre Boyer, president

17. America's reaction to the Haitian Revolution. According to writer John Loewen in his *Lies My Teacher Told Me: Everything Your American History Textbook Got Wrong,* American foreign policy toward Haiti can be summed up as follows:

> After the Revolution, many Americans expected our example would inspire other peoples. It did. Our young nation got its first chance to help in the 1790s, when Haiti revolted against France. Whether a president owned slaves seems to have determined his policy toward the second independent nation in the hemisphere. George Washington did, so his administration loaned hundreds of thousands of dollars to the French planters in Haiti to help them suppress their slaves. John Adams did not, and his administration gave considerable support to the Haitians. Jefferson's presidency marked a general retreat from the idealism of the Revolution. Like other slave owners, Jefferson preferred a Napoleonic colony to black republic in the Caribbean. In 1801 he reversed U.S. policy toward Haiti and secretly gave France the go-ahead to reconquer the island. In so doing, the United States not only betrayed its heritage, but also acted against its own self-interest. For if France had indeed been able to retake Haiti, Napoleon would have maintained his dream of an American empire. The United States would have been hemmed in by France to its west, Britain to its north, and Spain to its south.[266]

Latin America

1. Dominican Republic

The authors of *Revolutionary Freedoms* say the following:

> In 1844, after twenty-two years of Haitian rule, Santo Domingo, gained its independence from Haiti. However,

while the story has been documented, it seems that entire story has not been widely disseminated.[267]

It is important to remember that after its independence at the beginning of the nineteenth century, in its desire to make sure neither Spain nor France returned to Hispaniola, Haiti occupied Spanish Santo Domingo (the present-day Dominican Republic), and slavery was abolished on the entire island. In 1844, after 22 years of Haitians' rule, the Dominicans gained their independence from Haiti. Later, when Spain re-annexed Santo Domingo, Dominicans turned to Haiti to end Spanish domination. However, official Dominican history often omits this part of the story, and Independence Day for most Dominicans means from the Haitians, not the Spanish.[268]

In fact the Dominican Republic owes a debt to Haiti for freeing it more than once. Haitians, on the other hand, would rather starve than be colonized.

Economic factors are a primary reason why Dominican Republic president Pedro Santana concludes a treaty with Spain, whereby the Dominican state reverts back to a colony. It is the only Latin American state ever to do so. Haitian leaders, fearing the return of Spanish power to the island, welcome Dominican exile leaders and support them when they commence military operations in 1863, known as the Restoration War. The rebels are led by General Ulises Heureaux, of Haitian origin and former president of the Dominican Republic, and Gregorio Luperón.[269]

The war drags on until 1865, when the Spanish quit the island. The restoration is proclaimed on August 16, 1865.[270]

2. **Mexico**

"In November 1813, Joseph Savary and his men [500 Haitians soldiers] joined Mexican rebels fighting for their nation's independence."[271]

3. **Venezuela and Colombia**

Indeed, the independence of Venezuela and Colombia was partly won by the bravery of negro and mulatto soldiers fighting under Bolivar, Paez, and Sucre. And Bolivar was helped most materially during the critical years of his struggle (1814–16) by the assistance in men, arms, and money –two expeditions in all—granted to him by General Pétion, who was then ruling the southern part of the Negro republic of Haiti.[272]

For the seven ships, 250 men, guns and provisions that Pétion provided Bolívar for his campaign, the Haitian leader demanded that Bolívar liberate the slaves in whatever land he took from Spain.[273]

World War I

1. **Eugene Jacques Bullard,** the Black Swallow of Death, was the first black fighter pilot in the world.[274] He was also the only black pilot in World War I.[275] He was known as "The Black Swallow of Death" because of the bravery he displayed on missions.[276] During the start of World War I, he joined the French Foreign Legion and in time became a corporal. He received the Croix de Guerre for his bravery as an infantryman in combat.[277] Bullard was of Haitian descent, for his ancestors had been slaves of French refugees from the Haitian revolution.[278] In 1959, the French honored him with the Knight of the Legion of Honor.[279]

2. **Charles Terres Weymann** (See "Pilots" chapter.)

3. **Admiral Hamilton Killick** achieved immortality on September 6, 1902 when he chose death and went down with his navy gunship *La Crete-a-Pierrot* rather than surrender to the Germans in Gonaives, Haiti. Upon President Tirésis Simon Sam's precipitous departure from Haiti, it became a political struggle between Nord Alexis and

Anténor Firmin to see who would take power in Port-au-Prince. "Admiral Killick, who commanded the patrol ship La Crête-à-Pierrot, supported Firmin and consequently had confiscated a German ship [Mariomania], transporting arms and munitions to the provisional Haitian government of Alexis."[280]

> Not sharing the position of Hamilton Killick, the government ordered another German warship, the Panther, to seize the Crête-à-Pierrot. But it didn't realize the determination and courage of Admiral Killick. At Gonaïves, the Germans had the surprise of their life. When the German ship appeared off the roadstead of the city, Admiral Killick, who was then ashore, hurried on board and ordered his whole crew to abandon the ship. The Germans did not understand this maneuver. Once the sailors were out of danger, Admiral Killick together with Dr. Coles [the surgeon of the ship], who also did not want to leave, wrapped himself in the Haitian flag, like Captain Laporte in 1803, and blew the Crête-à-Pierrot up by firing at the munitions. The German sailors did not even dream of an act so heroic.[281]

World War II

1. **Haitian Tuskegee Airmen.** In the 1940s, a Haitian paper ran an ad calling for pilots. We know for sure that six (there could have been more) Haitians responded to this ad and went to train at the Tuskegee Institute in Alabama. Some of these men were already in the Haitian army or air force.[282] Their names follow:

> a. **Sergeant/Lieutenant Ludovic Audant** was born in Port-au-Prince, Haiti, and completed the training with "outstanding student" merit. He aided the United States in patrolling the Caribbean Sea against enemy submarines until the end of the war.[283]

b. **Philippe Célestin** (nicknamed **Phito)** graduated from Ecole Militaire D'Haiti. Unfortunately, he was a washout and did not make it thought the rigid training. He succeeded in the primary stage and the basic stage but was eliminated during the upper-basic stage. Later he was arrested for insubordination under Francois Duvalier and never seen again.[284]

c. **Raymond Cassagnol** worked as a mechanic for the Haitian air force. He was honored in Italy for his contribution to World War II as a Tuskegee Airman gun-pilot. Decades later, he, Guilbaud, and Pasquet were acknowledged by the United States. He is the only surviving Haitian Tuskegee Airman alive today and was a special guest at the inauguration of President Barack Obama in 2009.[285]

d. **Eberle J. Guilbaud** was born in Port-au-Prince, Haiti, and was barely twenty-five when he completed training at the Tuskegee Institute in April 1944. He survived the war, but he and others died during plane hijacking "when about 15 years later opponents of the Duvalier government hijacked a Haitian plane that was heading to Cuba."[286]

e. **Sergeant/Lieutenant Pelissier Nicolas** graduated from Ecole Militaire D'Haiti and graduated from Tuskegee Institute in Alabama.[287]

f. **Alix Pasquet** was a member of the Haitian air force when he was recruited by the United States. His graduation was delayed due to illness.[288]

Pilot graduates from the Tuskegee Flight School listed in alphabetical order by last names, along with class number, graduation date, rank held at Tuskegee, serial number, and hometown follow:[289]

- Audant, Ludovic F. 44-B-SE 2/8/1944 Port-au-Prince, Haiti

- Cassagnol, Raymond 43-G-SE 7/28/1943 unknown, Haiti
- Guilbaud, Eberle J. 44-D-TE 4/15/1944 Port-au-Prince, Haiti
- Nicolas, Pelissier C. 44-B-TE 2/8/1944 Port-au-Prince, Haiti
- Pasquet, Alix 43-H-SE 8/30/1943 Haiti

2. "During World War II (1939–1945), after the Japanese bombing of Pearl Harbor in 1941, Haiti's president, Elie Lescot, declared war on Japan, Germany, and Italy. At the request of the United States, and in exchange for aid, Haiti hosted a detachment of the U.S. Coast Guard and provided food to Allied forces during the war."[290]

Left: Eugene Jacques Bullard (known as: The black swallow of death) Right: Alix Pasquet

Top Left: Philippe Celestin, Raymond Cassagnol, Capt. Graham (Basic Instructor), and Alix Pasquet. Top Right: Raymond Cassagnol. Bottom Left: Raymond Cassagnol, Phillipe Célestin, and Alix Pasquet. Bottom Right: Eberle Guilbaud

Refuge Seekers

1. Latin America

Twice did Bolivar, the Liberator of South America, find a secure refuge at Aux Cayes in Southern Haiti when all other neutral ports were closed to him. Yet at a later date, he showed himself most ungrateful to the Haitians, affecting to ignore the existence of their republic and omitting to send to them, as well as to all the other recently enfranchised states, any diplomatic representative of his new government.[291]

2. "From 1830, when the revolt against Russian occupation of Poland started, some Jewish families fled to Haiti, where they generally joined the upper classes."[292]

3. **World War II**

In 1937, the Haitian government began issuing passports and visas to approximately 100 Eastern European Jews escaping Nazi persecution. According to the Joint Distribution Company, "Haiti played a small, yet critical, role in saving Jewish lives during the darkest chapter in the Jewish story." The JDC's organizational records show that up to 150 Jewish refugees managed to escape Europe to come to Haiti. Unfortunately, though, it seems that more Jews were unable to acquire visas to Haiti due to the cost. Prof. David Bankier, of the Institute of Contemporary Jewry at the Hebrew University of Jerusalem, said that after 1938, "the cost [of a visa] was outrageous: If you wanted to go to Haiti, you had to pay $5,000."[293]

4. "During World War II, Haiti was one of the few countries in the world to open its doors to Jewish refugees, but most Jews emigrated after the war ended."[294]

17

Miscellaneous

1. In 1789, there were nearly five hundred thousand slaves in St. Domingue, and the annual slaves imported reached thirty thousand, half of whom were African-born.[295]

2. **John P. Burr** was reputed to be the son of Aaron Burr, third vice president of America, and his Haitian-born governess. A New Jersey native, Burr, who was a hairdresser, was a very active member of his community. He promoted emigration to Haiti, served as agent for the *Liberator, and* protested disfranchisement. He sheltered fugitive slaves and aided those charged with treason in the Christiana Riot of 1851.[296] He was a stalwart of the American Moral Reform Society; he helped in the publishing of its journal, the *National Reformer*. Burr also took part in the national convention movement of the 1830s and in the organization of the Pennsylvania Anti-Slavery Society. The struggle against slavery was a family affair for his wife, Hetty, a dressmaker, and their children, daughter J. Matilda and sons John E. and David, both barbers like their father. Burr had two other sons, Edward and Martin, who were carpenters.[297] Burr was also an officer of two community institutions, the Mechanic's Enterprise Hall and the Moral Reform Retreat, a refuge for black alcoholics.[298]

3. **Jacquotte Delahaye**, a seventeenth-century Haitian female pirate or buccaneer born in St. Domingue, was the daughter of a Haitian mother and a French father. Her mother is said to have died during childbirth, and this difficult birth left her brother suffering from mild brain damage. After the murder of her father, Delahaye took up piracy to support herself and her brother.[299] She was called "Back from the Dead Red" (she had striking red hair), a name she received after faking her death to avoid government pursuit, and she would

live life as a man for years before returning to piracy. She led a gang of a hundred pirates, and in 1656, she and her follow pirates took over a small Caribbean island from the Spanish and called it the Freebooter Republic. Delahaye would die in a shootout while defending her republic.[300] Delahaye is thought to have sailed for a time alongside fellow pirate Ann Dieu-Le-Veut.[301] Delahaye, who never married, had this to say about men: "I couldn't love a man who commands me any more than I could love one who lets himself be commanded by me."[302]

4. **William de Fleurville (Florville)** was the Haitian barber of Abraham Lincoln, also known as "Billy the Barber." He immigrated to Baltimore in 1829 and learned the barbering trade.[303] He arrived in New Salem in 1831 and set up shop in 1832, where he met President Lincoln. The two men became lifelong friends. He opened his barbershop in "a new building opposite the north front of the State House." His shop, the first barbershop in Springfield, was located on Adams Street between Sixth and Seventh, "just below the office of the Mayor." It was Lincoln's second home.[304] He was a man of musical talent, for he was a "flute and violin player, a considerable philanthropist in the growing frontier community, and a composer of seriocomic verses that he published in the *Illinois State Journal*. "Billy will always be found on the spot/With razor keen and water smoking hot/He'll clip and dress your hair, and shave with ease/ And leave no effort slack his friends to please.""[305] He was Lincoln's barber for twenty-four years as well as his neighbor for a time and the guardian of the Lincoln home when the family was in Washington.[306] Fleurville used Lincoln at various times as an attorney. Some of these dealings included estate transactions. When William de Fleurville died in 1868, he was among Springfield's wealthiest citizens.[307]

The letter below by Lincoln is for one of these real-estate transactions. This letter was found and copied from a b-n.com article by Ruth Cobb entitled "History & Mystery: Wall Art in Downtown Bloomington (Who Are These People, and Why Are They on the Wall?)."[308]

Bloomington, Sept. 27, 1852

C.R. Welles, Esq.
Dear Sir:

I am in a little trouble here—I am trying to get a decree for our "Billy the Barber" for the conveyance of certain town lots sold to him by Allin Gridley and Prickett—I made you a party, as administrator of Prickett, but the Clerk omitted to put your name in the writ, and so you are not served—Billy will blame me, if I do not get the thing fixed up this time—If, therefore you will be so kind as to sign the authority below, and send it to me, by return mail, I shall be greatly obliged, and will be careful that you shall not be involved, or your rights waived by it—

Yours as ever
A. Lincoln

One of the descendants of Fleurville researched the family tree and determined, "On the same branch of the family tree as De Fleurville, they found a great-great uncle, George Richardson, who was falsely accused of raping a white woman in one of the incidents that set off the Springfield Race Riot."[309] One of the "lasting consequences of the riot was its impetus in getting white reformers such as Jane Addams and black civil rights activists such as W.E.B. DuBois to create the National Association for the Advancement of Colored People (NAACP), one year later following an interracial conference in upstate New York."[310]

5. **Joseph Phillippe Lemercier Laroche.** Many have heard the stories of the families on the *Titanic*, but how many know of the only black passenger? This traveler was Haitian native Joseph Phillippe Lemercier Laroche. Eighty years after the 1912 tragedy, the world heard his story, thanks in part to the Chicago Museum of Science and Industry, host to the largest *Titanic* exhibit ever, and the Titanic

Historical Society.[311] Laroche was born in Cap Haitian on May 26, 1889 to a powerful family. His uncle was Dessalines M. Cincinnatus Leconte, president of Haiti. He studied engineering in Beauvais, France. After earning his degree, he married Juliette Lafargue, the daughter of a local wine seller, in 1908. Although he was well educated and spoke French and English fluently, he could not get a job due to his color. He had two daughters, Simonne and Louise (born prematurely and sickly), and he tired of having to rely on his father-in-law for financial help. He decided to take his family back home to Haiti. This trip was hastened due to the fact that his wife was now pregnant with their third child. Upon hearing the news that her son wanted to return home and wanted to meet his family, Laroche's mother bought tickets on the French liner *La France* as a homecoming gift. The family, however, exchanged these tickets for second-class tickets on *Titanic* once they found out that their children would not be permitted to dine with them on the *La France*.[312] The family boarded the doomed ship nicknamed "Palace of the Sea" on Wednesday, April 10, 1912, for a five-day crossing to New York. While on board, he made it clear that his family was second class to no one, and they enjoyed many of the spoils of the first-class passengers.[313]

"Historians agree that Laroche was calm and heroic" during the night of on April 15, 1912, when he loaded his wife and children on what historians believe to be Lifeboat number fourteen. While he and some 1,500 others went down with the *Titanic*, his body was never found. His wife returned to France with their children and gave birth to a son, Joseph Phillippe Lemercier Laroche Jr., "bearing a striking resemblance to his handsome father," a week before Christmas 1912. In 1918, six years after his death, White Star Line (insurance company) awarded Juliette Laroche 150,000 francs ($22,119 in 1918 money and about $254,374 in today's money), which she used to open a fabric-dyeing business. Ms. Laroche died in 1980. Their daughters never married. Simonne died in 1973, and Louise in 1998, and their son, Joseph, died in 1987. Laroche Jr. married a

French woman named Claudine. They had three children, two boys and a girl. His children still live in Paris.[314]

6. Many Haitians fled Haiti during the Haitian Revolution for America, both free blacks and French-speaking whites from St. Domingue. Many of these immigrants took their slaves with them. Many settled in Philadelphia, New York, Norfolk, Baltimore, Wilmington, and New Orleans. They established themselves in these cities as caterers, restaurateurs, cabinetmakers, undertakers, coffin makers, dressmakers, and hairdressers. For example, Peter Augustine and St. John Appo won national recognition as caterers and confectioners in Philadelphia. Appo's wife became famous for her ice cream. Theodore Duplessis became known in New York for his exquisite ice cream.[315]

7. **Berny Martin** was born in Port-au-Prince, Haiti. He is a fashion designer who is the founder and CEO of Catou; he is also the founder of Midwest Fashion Week (MFW). His line of clothing is an internationally recognized line of men and women's professional wear. He started his label in 2002 and named it Catou after his grandmother Elizabeth Catou Loiseau.[316]

8. Did you know that whites who came to St. Domingue came looking for riches? Some whites would gain wealth by marrying women of color with money. Historian J. A. Rogers proclaims the following:

> Impoverished French noblemen would come to Haiti, marry a rich mulatto girl, take her to France, and with her money re-establish his ancestral line. Pons, wrote, "French noblemen went to the colonies for the express purpose of repairing, by a matrimonial connection, a fortune wrecked by losses or misconduct. In these cases they despised prejudice. They cared nothing about color, provided it was not absolutely black. Riches were the great desiderata and made up for everything else. They returned to France with their tawny

escorts, where their Creole birth detracted nothing from their consequence in polite society." Some white men who married the mulatto girls did not even take the trouble to return to France.[317]

9. To honor and remember the native population, "Haitians pay tribute to the Arawaks each year; at Carnival time, some disguise themselves as Arawaks and dance their dance."[318]

10. Child prodigy Mabou Loiseau, a Haitian American from Queens, New York, at the age of five does the following:

- speaks seven languages—French, Creole, English, Spanish, Mandarin, Arabic, and Russian
- plays six musical instruments—harp, clarinet, violin, guitar, drum, and piano
- dances both tap and ballet
- engages in ice-skating and swimming

The parents of this girl wonder spend $1,500 a week on tutors and lessons. Her father works sixteen hours a day to pay for his daughter's activities. Loiseau's mother, a piano teacher, states, "All the sacrifices in the world (are worth it) for her. Furniture is not important. Education is." Their hard work is paying off for their daughter, who scored in the ninety-ninth percentile on the city test to enter gifted and talented schools.[319] We can only watch and wait to see what her future holds.

18

Pilots

A list of Haitian pilots is also included in the War World II section of chapter 16.

1. **Leon Parris,** "a Haitian, was the first man of African descent to fly long distance, over 2,400 miles, from New York to Haiti, in April 1932."[320]

2. **Charles Terres Weymann** was born in Port-au-Prince, Haiti, on August 2, 1889 to a Haitian mother and American father. His mother's family was very wealthy, and at some point they moved to France. He obtained his US nationality through his father.[321] He was fluent in Creole, French, and English.[322] Weymann was an aviation pioneer. He received his pilot's license in 1909 with the American Aero Club and was given the number twenty-four. He completed and was successful in major European aviation events in a variety of aircraft, and he won the Gordon Bennett Cup at Eastchurch, on the Isle of Sheppey in 1911. This event was reported in the *Automobile Topics* as follows:

> For the second time a lone American entry has been successful in the greatest aviation speed event of the year, Charles Terres Weymann, representing the United States, in a French Nieuport monoplane, winning the third contest for the Coupe International D'Aviation on July 1 in dashing style at the aviation field at Eastchurch, Sheppey Island, England. He covered the 93.2-mile course in 71 minutes 36 1-5 seconds, an average speed of 78 miles an hour.[323]

During the war, he was test pilot for Nieuport, a French airplane manufacturer. He was honored with the rank of chevalier of the Legion of Honor and recipient of the Croix de Guerre. Weymann invented "a flexible automobile body based on aircraft design principles and by 1921 he had built his first motor vehicle body prototype in his small Carrosserie Weymann at No. 20 Rue Troyon in Paris." He patented his invention, and the license was sold to over forty French brands and body shops. By 1926, Weymann had made a fortune on his patents. He boasted of 123 licensees worldwide.[324] He died in France in 1976.

19

Production

1. The plantation system of St. Domingue grew rapidly, and by the 1750s it was the leader in sugar production. It produced more sugar than all of Britain's West Indies colonies put together, leaving France in control of about 40 percent of the worldwide sugar trade and 60 percent of its coffee. The island's slave population was five hundred thousand or almost half of the total slave population in the Caribbean. France largely owes its economic growth and industrial development to the blacks of St. Domingue.[325]

In 1767, St. Domingue exported 123 million pounds of sugar, one million pounds of indigo, and two million pounds of coffee, along with animal hides, molasses, cocoa, and rum. By 1789, there were one thousand merchant ships carrying goods between St. Domingue and France, making up 67 percent of all French export and import trade.[326] In fact, the labor of St. Domingue blacks produced a combined annual export and import trade of $140 million, dwarfing that of the thirteen American colonies and even that of Spain's colonies.[327] Also in 1791, there were 792 sugar plantations, 2,180 coffee, 705 cotton, 3,097 indigo, 69 cocoa, and 632 raising subsistence crops. St. Domingue's exports to France alone totaled approximately $41 million, with the net worth of the colony put at $300 million according to historians Robert Debs Heinl and Nancy Gordon Heinl. It is no wonder that, with all this money being made, in France the common saying was "rich as a Creole."[328] Planters made so much money in St. Domingue they were called the "Lords of Haiti" while planters on Martinique were called "Gentlemen of Martinique" and those on Guadeloupe were known as "Good People of Guadeloupe." This great feat of production and wealth was possible due to the fact that human beings were being worked to death. For example, according to Ros, in 1791, the number of slaves stood at a minimum of 450,000 and a maximum of 500,000. Every year, four thousand ships delivered at least thirty thousand new blacks from Africa, but there were also years when between fifty thousand and one hundred thousand were delivered.[329]

2. In the field of business, Haitian entrepreneurs are changing the landscape economically and socially. For instance, Kreyol Essence, a Haiti-based company that offers an extensive array of luxury beauty products, currently has over fifty employees.[330] They plan on planting over forty thousand castor-oil plants and most likely will employ over three hundred people in the next few years. There is also thirty-two-year-old Haitian Canadian, Charles Stevens, who founded LS Cream Liqueur. Born in Montreal, Quebec, to Haitian parents, Stevens's LS Cream (Cremas) has proven to be a success, and this traditional Haitian liqueur has won the WSWA Tasting Competition, 2014 Spirit Gold award, and the San Francisco World Spirits Competition 2014 Silver Medal.[331] Then there is Leanna Archer, a Haitian American who at the age of nine, using her grandmother's secret formula for hair care, started her own company, Leanna, Inc., that produces hair and skincare products (http://www.leannashair.com/). In 2013, at age sixteen, Archer was a CEO of a company grossing over $100,000 a year in revenue. She also has a nonprofit organization called the Leanna Archer Education Foundation that provides education, meals, and a safe environment to underprivileged children in Haiti. At the age of thirteen, she became the youngest person ever to ring the NASDAQ opening bell.[332]

3. Barbancourt rum from Haiti is widely known as the "rum of connoisseurs." It has won competitions in Haiti, England, Belgium, Switzerland, Austria, Germany, USA, France, Italy, Portugal, and Holland.[333] The Barbancourt family has been making its rum liquors since 1765. Barbancourt rum has been winning awards since 1885 to 2009.[334]

Barbancourt has five classifications: three-star rum aged for four years, five-star rum aged for eight years, and the Réserve Spéciale. The Réserve du Domaine, aged for fifteen years, was once only for the family and close friends. It was sold publicly for the first time in the mid-1960s. The remaining classifications are Rhum Barbancourt White rum and Pango Rhum.[335]

4. Haiti's Prestige beer was a gold medalist at the World Beer Cup in 2000.[336]

20

Religion

Candidates for Canonization

1. **Henriette Dellile** was of Haitian descent. She was born in New Orleans in 1812 to a prosperous and influential family. She was the youngest of four children conceived out of wedlock by Marie Josephe Diaz and Jean Baptiste Lille Sarpy (Sarpi). In 1824, she met and was influenced by French nun Sister Marthe Fontier, who opened a school for girls of color in New Orleans. Henriette Dellile was impressed by her Christian faith and acts of charity to her black neighbors. Sister Marthe also taught Henriette the value of missionary work among her race. It was a lesson she learned well. By fourteen, she was a lay catechist, teaching slaves on plantations about Christianity and visiting the sick and the aged, along with catechizing poor freed blacks and slaves. Henriette Dellile, while working in church institutions, tried to become a postulant but was refused by both the Ursuline and Carmelite orders because of her skin color. Even though she could have passed for white, she never did, for she was proud of the fact that she was black. She was a woman of determination, faith, and a deep love for God. She and Juliette Gaudin, a free person of color and a Haitian Cuban, established a home for black elderly citizens of New Orleans. They bought a house to teach black religion classes, and by so doing, they were breaking the law, for at the time it was illegal to educate blacks. They educated free and enslaved African Americans. She, Juliette, and Miss Josephine Charles were the cofounders of the Sisters of

the Holy Family in New Orleans in 1842. It was the second Catholic religious order of African American women in the United States. The first was started by Mother Mary of the order Oblate Sisters of Providence founded in Baltimore in 1829 (see Mother Mary Elizabeth Lange). Henriette's convent was supported by wealthy Afro-Creoles, including activists of Haitian descent such as Thomy Lafon. She and the other sisters took their vows in 1852 before Pere Etienne Rousselon, a white French immigrant, and adopted a plain religious habit. She and her order provided nursing care and took in orphans.[337]

The Sisters of the Holy Family campaigned against the moral wrongs of society such as the custom of plaçage, a New Orleans practice where white men would make free light-complexioned black women their mistresses. This was a practice in which her family also took part. Henriette herself was groomed for this kind of lifestyle but rejected it at seventeen.[338] Henriette Dellile died on November 17, 1862. In her obituary, it was written, "The crowd gathered for her funeral testified by its sorrow how keenly felt was the loss of her who for the love of Christ had made herself the humble servant of slaves." In the 1960s, the sisters of her order began exploring the possibility of canonization for her, and by 1989, they formally opened their cause to the Vatican. A movie on her life was made in 2001 starring Vanessa Williams; it premiered on cable's Lifetime.[339] If canonized, Henriette Dellile will be the first native-born black American saint. On November 18, 2001, a commemorative plaque was unveiled, featuring

Henriette DeLille and Juliette Gaudin, commemorating the November 21 Founder's Day of the Sisters of the Holy Family. Seventy sisters of the order attended the ceremony along with a rousing gospel mass.[340]

2. **Mother Mary Elizabeth Lange** was a Haitian-born nun who founded the Sisters of Oblate of Providence in Baltimore in 1829. During the slave uprising, Elizabeth Clarisse Lange and her family left Haiti and fled to Cuba, becoming refugees

like thousands of their fellow countrymen. Her father was a man of some financial means and social standing who may have also been French. Her mother was Creole. In the early 1800s, she left Santiago, Cuba, and in 1813, Providence directed her to Baltimore, Maryland, which at the time had a great influx of French-speaking Catholic San Domingans (Haitians) in their refugee settlement. This brave, educated young woman arrived in Maryland with the wealth her father left her and set out to help her fellow refugees and their children. With her money and home, she started to educate these children for free. Children were schooled in academic subjects and the Catholic faith. They were also taught music, the classics, and fine art. The children were also involved in choirs, concerts, recitals, and competitions for medals and awards in various subjects. Annual examinations were given by faculty members of St. Mary's and Loyola Colleges, according to Brinkmann. Mother Lange did this for ten years with the aid of her friend Marie Magdaline Balas (later Sister Frances, OSP).[341]

Her charitable works caught the attention of Archbishop James Whitfield of Baltimore. He was so impressed by her that he stated, "In this work is the finger of God." The archbishop sent Father James Hector Joubert, SS, who encouraged Mother Mary to found a new order dedicated specifically to the education of black children. He also provided spiritual direction, helped to raise money for their apostolate, and encouraged other black women to join them. Mother Mary founded and was superior general of the Oblate Sisters of Providence. She took her vows along with three other women on July 2, 1829 and took the name of Mary. Mother Mary was superior general of her order from 1829 to 1832 and from 1835 to 1841. This became the first black Roman Catholic order in the United States. It was also the first congregation of African Americans nuns in the history of the Catholic Church. The goal of this congregation was to educate, provide homes to orphans, and evangelize African Americans. They would buy, educate, and free slaves and at times admitted them into the congregation. The congregation would always be open to meeting the needs of the times. An example of this occurred during the cholera epidemic of 1832. The order nursed the terminally ill, and they all sheltered the elderly. When Archbishop Whitfield died and Father Joubert fell ill, the order was in near poverty and was ordered to disband by the new archbishop of Baltimore. This was out of the question for Mother Mary and her sisters. Instead of disbanding the order, they accepted work as domestics at St. Mary's Seminary. Their annual salaries of sixty dollars enabled them to continue their mission.[342]

Her life was not easy, and she faced poverty and racial injustice. She never lost faith and remained devoted. She served her congregation for fifty-three years. Mother Mary died on February 3, 1882 at the age of eighty-seven. Her funeral was held in the Cathedral of the Assumption of the Blessed Virgin. The order she founded is now 176 years old and can be found in twenty-five cities throughout the Americas in the United States, Cuba, Costa Rica, and the Dominican Republic. Steps are being taken to make Mother Lange a saint. She is one of three Haitians who are candidates for canonization.[343]

3. **Pierre Toussaint** was born a slave in Saint Domingue (present-day Haiti). Before the Haitian Revolution started, he was brought to New York by his slave owners in 1787. He was given his freedom in 1808. Before he was freed, he bought his sister, Rosalie, her freedom so she could marry and have free children. Toussaint also bought his wife, Juliet Noel, whom he married in 1811. Noel was a Haitian woman he had known for years. He and his wife had no children. However, they adopted Toussaint's niece Euphemia after the death of his sister. Unfortunately, Euphemia died of tuberculosis at fourteen. Her death was a great loss for the couple.[344] He also helped many other slaves buy their freedom.[345] He was a devout Catholic who attended mass

daily and strongly believed in helping his fellow men. His chartable deeds included the following:[346]

- He was instrumental in raising funds for the first Catholic orphanage.
- He began the city's first school for black children.
- He provided funds for the Oblate Sisters of Providence, a religious community of black nuns founded in Baltimore.
- He played a vital role in providing resources to erect Old Saint Patrick's Cathedral in Lower Manhattan.
- During a yellow-fever epidemic when many of the city's political leaders fled the city in search of healthier rural climates, Pierre Toussaint cared for the sick and the dying.

It is no wonder he is credited by many as being the father of Catholic Charities in New York. Toussaint was able to carry out his charitable works due to the fact that he was a successful entrepreneur who made his money as a hairdresser. High-society women spent $1,000 a year on their hairdos, enabling Toussaint to amass a good sum of money.[347] Pierre Toussaint died in 1853 and was buried in the yard of St. Peter's Church in New York City. Later his remains were moved to St. Patrick's Cathedral. Pope John Paul II declared Pierre Toussaint venerable in 1997, "thus placing him firmly on the road to becoming North America's first black saint."[348]

Holy People

1. **Mother Theresa Maxis Duchemin** was born in 1810 in Baltimore. She was the daughter of Haitian refugee Betsy Duchemin and British military officer Arthur Howard. Her parents were not married, and Theresa Maxis believed that her father never knew she existed. She was well educated and articulate in both French and English. At eighteen, she helped Mother Elizabeth Lange found the order of the Oblate Sister of Providence. When she was a part of this order, she served as both superior general and assistant to the superior general.

It was during service as a superior general that she met Louise Florent Gillet, CSSR, who was looking for religious women for schools in the then new state of Michigan. After thinking it over, Theresa Maxis agreed and found a new congregation in Monroe, and in 1845, she became one of the first three members of the sisters, Servants of the Immaculate Heart of Mary (IHM). Though slow in its developmental stages, it was well known for its educational work. Unfortunately, a jurisdictional dispute about the congregation arose in 1859 between the bishops of Philadelphia and Detroit. Theresa was held responsible for this by the bishop of Detroit, and she was removed as superior general. She was sent to the Pennsylvania foundation, which later became a separate branch of the congregation. As a result of many difficulties and misunderstandings, Mother Theresa was forced to leave this congregation and spent eighteen years in exile with the Grey nuns of Ottawa. She was allowed to return to the IHM congregation in West Chester, Pennsylvania, in 1885. She lived the remaining seven years of her life peacefully. The one painful deprivation she experienced was when Bishop William O'Hara refused to allow her to visit in Scranton or to receive regular communication from the sisters there. Mother Theresa died after a brief illness on January 14, 1892. The Maxis Foundation is named after her.[349]

2. **Juliette Gaudin** was a free person of color born in Cuba to Haitian refugees.[350] Juliette was educated by and attended Sister Ste. Marthe's School for Colored girls. She was taught reading, writing, arithmetic, geography, and religion.[351] She and Henriette Delille established a home for the black elderly citizens of New Orleans and bought a house to teach religion classes.[352] When her lifelong friend Mother Henriette died in 1862, Juliette succeeded her as mother superior.[353] Juliette Gaudin died on January 1, 1888.[354] On November 18, 2001, a commemorative plaque was unveiled featuring both women, commemorating the November 21 Founder's Day of the Sisters of the Holy Family.[355]

Bishop

1. **Bishop Guy A. Sansaricq** was the first Haitian-born Roman Catholic bishop in the United States. He was born on October 6, 1934 in Jérémie, Haiti.[356]

Traditional African Religion

1. **Boukman.** During the 1770s and 1780s, a new tactic replaced poisoning slave owners in St. Domingue, and this new tactic was outright violence. This started in the Fort Dauphin region in the north.[357] One of the great leaders of this new movement was a Creole slave born in Jamaica named Dutty (or Zamba) Boukman. He was physically described as being a very large and muscular man. It is not known if his name was really Boukman or not. He may have learned to read and write, and he was known to carry a book with him at all times. This could be the reason he was called "Boukman," meaning the man with a book, or the one who knows. He was believed to be a man of knowledge for his time—a *n'gan* (in Haitian, kréyòl hungan), a Vodou priest. Boukman was owned by a plantation owner named Turpin in St. Domingue. He became Turpin's *cocher* (coachman), and he was also given authority over his fellow slaves as a field commander due to his size. He would use his positions to gain influence over slaves, not only on his plantation but also on other plantations. On the night of August 14, 1791, legend states that he and his followers gathered in the woods of Bwa Kayiman (Bois Caiman) at Morne Rouge, in the northern part of St. Domingue.[358] Boukman held a Vodou ceremony in these woods; one individual who took part in this ceremony was mambo priestess Cécile Sesil Fatima.[359] Others who were present at this ceremony at Morne Rouge were Jorge Biassou, Jeannot Bullet, and Jean François (also known as Jean François Papillon).[360] Boukman led the service on behalf of two Vodou gods, Baron Samedi and Baron Lentrenc, who guarded and protected slaves.[361] They slaughtered a pig, ceremonially drank its blood, swore an oath of obedience to the leaders of the revolt,

and swore death to all foreigners or blancs.[362] An example of how important this oath was to the slaves was the slave Philibert, who was a trusted coachman that assassinated his owner, Odeluc. While Odeluc pled for his life, he reminded Philibert how good he was to him, to which Philibert replied, "That is true, but I have promised to kill you," and he did.[363] Boukman is said to have given the following invocation:

> Good Lord who made the sun that shines upon us, that riseth from the sea, Who maketh the storm to roar; and governeth the thunders. The Lord is hidden in the heavens, and there He watcheth over us. The Lord seeth what the *blanc* have done. Their god commandeth crimes, Ours giveth blessing upon us. The Good Lord hath ordained vengeance. He will give strength to our arms and courage to our hearts. He shall sustain us. Cast down the image of the god of the *blanc*, because he maketh the tears to flow from our eyes. Hearken unto Liberty That speaketh now in all our hearts.[364]

In *Written in Blood*, it states that on certain days known to devotees and priests of the Lwas, drums could be heard from the slaves' quarters, beating out different rhythms from those played during the day's work. There was a dance called *kabinda*; there were choruses and chants, the words half-African, half-French:

> We come from Ginen,
> We have no mother,
> We have no father,
> Marassa Eyo!
> Papa Danbala,
> Show us,
> Show us Dahomey again …[365]

Boukman promised his followers that on the night of August 22 they would receive a signal.[366] As promised, on August 22, 1791, soon after ten that night, the drums that were being played changed their beat.[367] Throughout the north, drumbeats could be heard. It was a signal to the slaves to attack.[368] Sugarcane fields, the woods, and plantations were simultaneously set on fire over a distance of hundreds of miles this night; it would be called "the night of fire" by author Martin Ros.[369]

2. **Cécile Sesil Fatiman** was a mambo priestess.[370] Fatiman was the daughter of an African woman and a Corsican prince. She took part in the ceremony in the woods of Bwa Kayiman (Bois Caiman) at Morne Rouge, in the northern part of St. Domingue, along with Boukman.[371] Her husband was Louis Michel (Jean-Louis) Pierrot, who commanded an indigenous battalion at Vertières during the revolution and later became president.[372]

3. **Princess Améthyste** (See "Slavery and Slave Revolts" section in chapter 16.)

4. **"Marie Laveau** was a legendary figure of Louisiana's Vodou practice. She was a free woman of color, a descendant of Haitians who migrated to New Orleans." She was married to two Haitian men: "Jacques Paris, a native of Jérémie, Saint Domingue," and fellow San Domingan, Captain Louis Christophe Duminye de Glapion, a member of a black battalion.[373]

21

Scholars and Writers

1. **Eustache** was "an unmixed Negro born in Haiti in 1773, awarded the Premier Prix de Vertu (a literary prize of the highest honor) by the French Academy in 1832."[374]

2. **Joseph Auguste Anténor Firmin** was born in Cap Haitian. He was a journalist, author, lawyer, cabinet minister, rebel, and a Haitian exile in St. Thomas, United States, Virgin Islands.[375] Best known for his 1885 work *De l'Égalité des Races Humaines* (*The Equality of Human Races*), which was produced as a response to French writer Count Arthur de Gobineau's work "Essai sur l'inegalite des Races Humaines" ("Essay on the Inequality of Human Races"). Gobineau's book was written to show the superiority of the Aryan race over not only the black race but people of color, which Gobineau's essay described as being inferior.[376] In his book, "Firmin argued the opposite—that 'all men are endowed with the same qualities and the same faults, without distinction of color or anatomical form. The races are equal.' He pioneered the integration of race and physical anthropology and is now considered by many as one of the fathers of anthropology and the first Black anthropologist."[377] What is interesting about *The Equality of Human Races* is that before Robert Kennedy stated that America would have a black president, it proves that Haitian-born Firmin in the nineteenth century said it first. In his chapter "The Role of the Black Race in the History of Civilization," he writes the following after

an admiring bow acknowledging the American abolitionist Wendell Phillips's praise and analysis of Haiti's defeat of the slave system and its influence on the abolition of slavery in the United States:[378]

> Appearances to the contrary, this big country is destined to strike the first blow against the theory of the inequality of the human races. Indeed, at this very moment, Blacks in the great federal republic have begun to play a prominent role in the politics of the various states of the American union. It seems quite possible that, in less than a century from now, a Black man might be called to head the government of Washington and manage the affairs of the most progressive country on earth, a country which will inevitably become, thanks to its agricultural and industrial production, the richest and most powerful in the world. These are not utopian musings. We only have to consider the increasing participation of Blacks in American society to cast aside our skepticism. Besides, we must remember that slavery in the United States was abolished only twenty years ago.[379]

In the dedication section of his book, Firmin stated that he hoped that his book "may inspire in all of the children of the Black race around the world the love of progress, justice, and liberty. In dedicating this book to Haiti I bear them all in mind, both the downtrodden of today and the giants of tomorrow."[380]

3. **Louis Félix Mathurin Boisrond-Tonnerre**, better known as simply Boisrond-Tonnerre, was a Haitian writer and historian who is best known for having served as Jean-Jacques Dessalines's secretary. Boisrond-Tonnerre was educated in Paris until 1798 when he returned to Haiti (Daut 56). He is the author of the 1804 Independence Act of Haiti, which formally declared Haiti's independence from the colonial rule of France. He is also known for his work chronicling the Haitian Revolution, *Mémoires pour Servir à l'Histoire d'Haïti.*

4. **Dany Laferrière** was honored with the Prix Médicis in 2009, France's literary prize, celebrating original writing for his novel *The Enigma of the Return*. The Haitian-born Laferrière was the first Canadian honored with this literary prize since 1966.[381]

5. **Victor Séjour**, one of France's most creative and popular playwrights, was born in New Orleans of Haitian parentage. His father, Louis, was a Haitian immigrant, and his mother, Héloïse, was a free woman of color from New Orleans.[382] Séjour was the secretary of Prince Napoleon, later Napoleon III. Needless to say, he had a great deal of influence at the French court.[383]

Conclusion

The history of Haiti is beset with tragedy and disaster, with the most recent calamity being the earthquake of 2010. However, all this turmoil has not stopped the glory of the Haitian people from shining through. As one can see from the achievements listed in these pages, the contributions of Haiti and her children did not just start or end with their fight for independence but continues today in Haiti and throughout the world. The children of the Pearl of the Caribbean are still showing signs of promise for the future.

About the Author

I hold advanced degrees in architecture technology, library information science, and urban studies. I have worked in libraries for more than twenty years and continue to supervise and instruct at academic libraries. One of the factors that motivated my decision to study library science was my desire to be exposed to books and knowledge that I could not find in other fields. I started studying African history rigorously during my first job in academia eighteen years ago, and the wealth of knowledge that I discovered about the black race was so amazing that I spent the next ten years collecting data on black people from around the world. In 2014, I decided that I needed to share all that I had discovered; therefore, I created the website SankofaArchives.com to help people of African descent discover positive images of their ancestors and understand their contributions to world history.

While my knowledge of African and European history was advanced, my knowledge of my own cultural background was limited. I am Haitian American. I was born and raised in America; however, both of my parents are Haitian born and raised. Growing up in America, my culture, as portrayed by the media, seemed to center only on voodoo practitioners or on people escaping from Haiti by boat. I cannot count the number of times I have been asked, "Do you practice voodoo?" and many who have asked me this question know that I am a professed Roman Catholic. In the 1980s, it was even worse for Haitians, for "all Haitians had AIDS." Positive images of Haitians were extremely rare.

Yes, Haiti is an impoverished country that is far removed from its days of glory. However, it is still an impressive grand dame with its colorful marketplaces, tap-taps, and artwork, which is sold on the sidewalks. One cannot help but love her. My Haitian family members exposed my sister and me to the positive side of Haitian culture. I was lucky in that, from ten to the age of eighteen, I spent my summers in Haiti, where we would stay in beautiful hotels. Haiti's architecture is amazing. I was most impressed with the gingerbread-style hotels, such as the Kinam Hotel in Petionville, and I enjoyed visiting my grandfather's two-story shotgun house.

During my years of research, I came across bits and pieces of information about Haitians; this material not only surprised but also fascinated me. I, therefore, started trying to find information on my culture and the contributions of Haitian people to world history. I must say that this task was not easy. I quickly came to the realization that I needed to know not only the colonial name of Haiti, which was St. Domingue, but also the various spellings of it: Saint Domingue, Saint Dominique, and San-Domingue, just to name a few. I also found that researchers would confuse Saint Domingue with Santo Domingo and classify Haitians as Dominicans. Even the name Haiti has various spelling, such as Ayiti and Hyiti. Finding information about Haitian individuals in history was no easier, as Haitians were frequently written about as if they were Spanish or French. Those born in America were now Americans, and hardly any mention of their cultural background was ever made. This was true even for those Haitians who came to America as adults.

My research also revealed that many Haitians hide their cultural heritage because of the negativity surrounding the country. For example, when Haiti was devastated by a massive earthquake in 2010, this devastation, according to televangelist Pat Robertson, was said to be a curse because of a Haitian pact with the devil. Robertson stated, "Something happened a long time ago in Haiti, and people might not want to talk about it … They were under the heel of the French. You know Napoleon III, or whatever. And they got together and swore a pact to the devil. They said, 'We will serve you if you'll get us free from the French.' True story. And so, the devil said, 'Okay, it's a deal.'" We, as Haitians, always have to defend our culture, and this becomes tiring. It is often easier to just say nothing at all.

I wrote this book so that Haitians worldwide can read about the contributions of Haiti and her children. I wanted it to be composed of quick facts and pertinent details and not be weighed down with minutiae like most history books are. I hope that it will encourage others to do their own research on Haitian culture. Most of all, I hope this book will cause Haitians born outside of Haiti to take pride in our ancestors and our culture.

Appendix

List of Heads of State of Haiti
(1791–Present)
Acting, King, Emperors, Interims, Presidents,
Provisional Governments

Jean-Jacques Dessalines	(1804–1806) Emperor of Haiti	Assassinated
Henri Christophe	(1807–1820) King of Haiti North	Suicide
Alexandre Pétion	(1807–1818) South	Died in office
Jean-Pierre Boyer	(1818–1843)	Overthrown
Charles Ainé (Rivière) Hérard	(1843–1844)	Overthrown
General Philippe Guerrier	(1844–1845)	Died in office
General Jean Louis Pierrot	(1845–1846)	Overthrown
Jean-Baptiste Riché	(1846–1847)	Died in office
Faustin Soulouque	(1847–1859) Emperor of Haiti	Overthrown
Fabre Nicolas Geffard	(1859–1867)	Overthrown
Major Sylvain Salnave	(1867–1870) President for life	Executed
Nissage Saget	(1870–1874)	Full term
Michel Dominique	(1874–1876)	Overthrown
Boisrond Canal	(1876–1879)	Overthrown
Louis Etienne Félicité Lysius Salomon	(1879–1888)	Overthrown
François Denys Légitime	(1888–1889)	Overthrown
Florville Hyppolite	(1889–1896)	Died in office
Tirésias Simon-Sam	(1896–1902)	Full term
Pierre Nord-Alexis	(1902–1908)	Overthrown
Antoine Simon	(1908–1911)	Overthrown
Cincinnatus Leconte	(1911–1912)	Died in office
Tancrede Auguste	(1912–1913)	Died in office
Michel Oreste	(1913–1914)	Overthrown
Oreste Zamor	(1914–1915) for one month	Overthrown
Davilmer Theodore	(1915) for four months	Overthrown
Vilbrun Guillaume Sam	(1915)	Assassinated

Philipppe Sudre Dartinguenave	(1915–1922)	Full term
Louis Borno	(1922–1930)	Full term
Louis Eugene Roy	(1930)	Interim president
Stenio Vincent	(1930–1941)	Full term
Elie Lescot	(1941–1946)	Overthrown
Franck Lavaud	(1946) First term	Chairman Military Executive Committee
Dumarais Estime	(1946–1950)	Overthrown
Franck Lavaud	1950 Second term	Chairman Military Executive Committee
Paul Eugene Magloire	(1950–1956)	Overthrown
Joseph Nemours Pierre-Louis	(1956–1957) one month and ten days	Provisional government
Franck Sylvain	(1957) two months	Provisional government
Léon Cantave	(1957)	Army chief of general staff
Daniel Fignolé	(1957)	Overthrown
Antonio Thrastybule Kébreau	(1957)	Chairman Military Council
François "Papa-Doc" Duvalier	(1957–1971) President for life	Died in office
Jean-Claude Duvalier	(1971–1986) President for life	Overthrown
General-President Henri Namphy	(1986–1988) First term	Chairman National Council—full term
Leslie F. Manigat	(1988)	Overthrown
General-President Henri Namphy	(1988) Second term	Overthrown
Matthieu Prosper Avril	(1988–1990)	Overthrown
Hérard Abraham	(1990)	Interim president
Ertha Pascal-Trouillot	(1990–1991)	Provisional government
Jean-Bertrand Aristide	(1991) First term	Overthrown—three years exile
Raoul Cédras	(Oct 1, 1991–Oct 8, 1991)	Acting leader of military junta; de facto leader to October 12, 1994
Joseph Nérette	(1991–1992)	Provisional government
Marc Bazin	(1992–1993)	Acting
Jean-Bertrand Aristide	(1993–1994) Second term	In exile but recognized in Haiti
Émile Jonassaint	(1994)	Provisional government
Jean-Bertrand Aristide	(1994–1996) Third term	President
René Préval	(1996–2001) First term	President
Jean-Bertrand Aristide	(2001–2004) Fourth term	President

Boniface Alexandre	(2004–2006)	Provisional government
René Préval	(2006–2011) Second term	President
Michel Joseph Martelly	(2011–)	Full term

Endnotes

Basic Facts

1   Raphaël Paquin and José Brax, eds., *History of Haiti 1492–2000 in French and English* (Pétion-Ville, Haiti: Sogebel, 2002), 19.
2   Paquin and Brax, 22.
3   CIA: Haiti, The World FactBook, retrieved August 27, https://www.cia.gov/library/publications/the-world-factbook/geos/ha.html.
4   Robert Chaudenson, *Creolization of Language and Culture* (London, UK: Routledge, 2001), 26.
5   CIA and Graves, 55.
6   Roseline NgCheong-Lum and Leslie Jermyn, *Haiti* (New York: Marshall Cavendish Benchmark, 2006), 7.
7   Michael R. Hall, *Historical Dictionary of Haiti* (Lanham: Scarecrow Press, 2012), 182.
8   Anthony Appiah and Henry Louis Gates, *Africana: The Encyclopedia of the African and African American Experience,* vol. 3, second ed. (New York: Basic Civitas Books, 2005), 118.

The Natives of Haiti

9   Franklin W. Knight, *The Caribbean* (New York: Oxford University Press, 1990), 7.
10 Bartolomé De Las Casas, *A Short Account of the Destruction of the Indies,* ed. and trans. Nigel Griffin, with an introduction by Anthony Pagden (London: Penguin Group, 1992), 18.
11 Ibid., 18.
12 Ibid., 20.
13 Ibid., 21.
14 Dr. Jan Carew, *Rape of Paradise, Columbus and the Birth of Racism in the Americas* (Brooklyn, New York: A&B Books Publishers, 1994), 246.
15 Bartolomé De Las Casas, 21–22.
16 Ibid., 22–23
17 Dr. Jan Carew, 225.
18 Ibid., 157–158.
19 Ibid.
20 Ibid., 12.

21 Ibid., 11.

22 Guy Henry and Clair Hershey, "Cassava in South America and the Caribbean," *CAB International*, 2002, *Cassava: Biology, Production and Utilization*, 2002, http://www.ciat.cgiar.org/downloads/pdf/cabi_05ch2.pdf.

23 Irving Rouse, *The Tainos Rise & Decline of the People Who Greeted Columbus* (New Haven: Yale University Press, 1992), 13.

24 Ibid.

25 Ibid., 119.

26 Ibid.

27 Ibid.

28 Ibid., 16.

29 Bartolomé De Las Casas, *The Devastation of the Indies: A Brief Account*, trans. Herma Briffault (Baltimore: John Hopkins University Press, 1992), 32.

The Africans

30 Mary C. Truck, *Haiti, Land of Inequality* (Minneapolis: Lerner Publication Company, 1999), 35.

31 Selden Rodman, *Haiti the Black Republic, The Standard Guide to Haiti* (Old Greenwich: Devin-Adair Publishers, 1984), 8.

32 Robert Debs Heinl and Nancy Gordon Heinl, *Written in Blood* (Lanham: University Press of America, 2005), 29.

33 Martin Ros, *Night of Fire, the Black Napoleon and the Battle for Haiti* (United States: Da Capo Press, 1994), 12.

34 David Geggus, "The British Government and The Saint-Domingue Slave Revolt, 1791–1793," *The English Historical Review* 96, no. 379 (1981): 285–305.

35 Richards Watts, "Dessalines, Jean-Jacques," in *Africana: The Encyclopedia of the African and African American Experience*, 2nd ed., vol. 2, Catimbó–Giovanni (Oxford University Press, 2005), 368.

Architecture and Monuments

36 Kerry A. Graves, *Haiti* (Mankato, Minnesota: Bridgestone Books, 2002), 6.
    – Lizabeth Paravisini-Gebert, *Literature of the Caribbean* (Westport, CT: Greenwood Press, 2008), 36.

37 Schomburg Center for Research in Black Culture, "The Consequences of the Haitian
        Migration," accessed March 12, 2012, http://www.inmotionaame.org/gallery/detail.cfm?migration=5&topic=9&id=464768&type=image&metadata=show&page.

38   Charles Philip Lazarus, *Jamaican History*, accessed March 31, 2011, http://joyousjam2.tripod.com/charleslazarus/index.html.

39   Charles P. Lazarus, *Jamaican History* February 2004, accessed March 31, 2011, http://www.joyousjam.info/jamaicanhistoryfebruary2004/id31.html.

40   Ibid.

41   "New York opens slave burial site: A burial ground for African slaves, which had been forgotten for almost two centuries, has been opened to the public in New York," *BBC News International Version*, October 6, 2007 accessed October 12, 2007, http://news.bbc.co.uk/2/hi/americas/7031142.stm.

42   Rodney Leon, AIA, NOMA, AARRIS Architects, accessed October 3, 2007, http://www.aarris.com/.

43   "Rodney Leon Tapped to Design Memorial for National Historic Landmark Winner to Create Memorial for 17th, 18th-Century Africans," US General Service Administration, Friday, April 29, 2005, accessed October 3, 2007, http://www.africanburialground.gov/Press_Releases/rodneyleon_042905.pdf.

44   Ibid.

45   "Haitian American Designer Helps Open African Burial Ground," HardbeatNews.Com Daily Caribbean Diaspora News, October 12, 2007, accessed October 12, 2007, http://www.hardbeatnews.com/editor/RTE/my_documents/my_files/details.asp?newsid=13820&title=Top%20Stories.

46   HABETAC The Haitian Bilingual/ESL Technical Assistance Center, *Haitian Historical and Cultural Legacy: A Journey Through Time: A Resource Guide for Teachers,* 1–2, accessed March 12, 2012,
         http://depthome.brooklyn.cuny.edu/habetac/Publications_files/Haitian-Historical.pdf.

Art and Culture

47   Régine Barjon, *Effectiveness of Aid in Haiti and How Private Investment Can Facilitate the Reconstruction,* written statement of Régine Barjon to the US Senate Subcommittees of Foreign Relations on International Development and Foreign Assistance and Western Hemisphere hearing entitled "Rebuilding Haiti in the Martelly Era," Thursday, June 23, 2011, accessed December 29, 2011, http://www.foreign.senate.gov/imo/media/doc/Simon-Barjon%20testimony.pdf.

48   Joseph D. Ketner and Robert S. Duncanson, *The Emergence of the African-American Artist: Robert S. Duncanson, 1821–1872* (Columbia: University of Missouri Press, 1993), 97.

49   Leslie M. Harris, *In the Shadow of Slavery: African Americans in New York City, 1626–1863* (Chicago: University of Chicago Press, 2003), 235, accessed February 25, 2013, http://hdl.handle.net/2027/heb.06703.

50   Carole Boyce Davies, *Encyclopedia of the African Diaspora: Origins, Experiences, and Culture,* vol. 1, A–C (Santa Barbara, CA: ABC-CLIO, 2008), 595–596.

51   Carol Bergman, *Sidney Poitier* (Los Angeles, CA: Melrose Square Pub., 1990), 26.

52   "Caribbean American Singer Maxwell in Line for Multiple Soul Train Awards," *Caribbean Today* (2009): 12, accessed January 13, 2012, http://search.proquest.com/docview/196934382?accountid=12142.

53   Boyce Davies, 150.

54   Garcelle Beauvais Biography, *Starpluse.com,* accessed January 13, 2012, http://www.starpulse.com/Actresses/Beauvais,_Garcelle/Biography/.

55   The Q: the Side Quddus' Official Website, accessed January 13, 2012, http://www.theqside.com/about-2.

56   Tyrone Edmond, Facebook.com, accessed January 13, 2012, http://www.facebook.com/pages/Tyrone-Edmond/103087859730938.

57   Yolanda Sangweni, "7 Things to Know About 'Hunger Games' Star Meta Golding," *Essence* (November 11, 2013), http://www.essence.com/2013/11/11/meta-golding-hunger-games-interview-7-things/.

Beauty Pageant Winners

58   Alejandro Guevara Onofre, "Miss Universe 2007 in Mexico is a profile about Miss Universe Pageant. In my opinion, I think that Miss Universe Pageant is a symbol of the modern woman in this century ..." *Buzzle.com,* accessed March 31, 2011, http://www.buzzle.com/articles/miss-universe-2007-mexico.html.

    – "15 Beauties in Miss Universe Spotlight," *Spokesman Review* (July 15, 1962), accessed March 31, 2011, http://news.google.com/newspapers?id=504pAAAAIBAJ&sjid=vOcDAAAAIBAJ&pg=5301,4829544&dq=evelyn-miot&hl=en.

59   Alejandro Guevara Onofre, "Haiti: The First Black Republic in the History," accessed March 31, 2011, http://www.voiceofarkansas.com/content/p/5031/catid/36/artid/3159.

60   Ibid.

61   "Marjorie Vincent, former Miss America, named TV anchor in Meridian, MS, for NBC-affiliate WGBC-TV—Brief Article," *Jet Magazine* 85, no. 6 (Dec. 6, 1993): 12.

– Lynn Norment, "Back-to-Back Black Miss Americas: Marjorie Judith Vincent Makes History When Crowned by Reigning Black Queen," *Ebony Magazine* XLVI, no. 2 (December 1990): 46–50.

62   Jake Pearson, "Daughter of Haitian Immigrants Vying to be 1st Miss Teen USA from N.Y in 30 yrs. Crown Would Be a Thing of Beauty," *New York Daily News,* Tuesday, March 29, 2011, 6.

63   *Miss New York TEEN USA 2011 Crowning Moments.mp4*, uploaded by blackwatervideo on Dec. 3, 2010, accessed March 31, 2011, http://www. youtube.com/watch?v=0jx-KzUFTgk.

64   Lilit Marcus, "Miss Haiti: Is Having a National Beauty Queen an Accomplishment?" *Huffington Post* online, August 20, 2010, accessed January 10, 2012,

      http://www.huffingtonpost.com/lilit-marcus/miss-haiti-is-having-a-na_b_687151.html.

      – Sarodj Bertin, *Haitian American Community Association*, accessed January 10, 2012,

      http://www.hacachicago.com/index.php?option= com_content&view=article&id=217.

Civil Rights

65   Steve Crowe, "Mary Ellen Pleasant: Unsung Heroine," *The New Crisis*, 16, no.1 (January/February 1999: 35.

66   Ibid.

67   Ibid.

Education

68   William Edward Burghardt DuBois, *The Autobiography of W. E. B. DuBois* (New York: International Publishers, 1971), 66.

69   "Dr. Carole Berotte Joseph Named President of Bronx Community College; Distinguished Educator Returns Home to CUNY," The City University of New York, accessed February 16, 2011, http://www1.cuny.edu/mu/ forum/2011/01/24/dr-carole-berotte-joseph-named-president-of-bronx-community-college-distinguished-educator-returns-home-to-cuny/

70   "Dr. Carole M. Berotte-Joseph First Haitian-American to Head Community College," *New York Carib News* XXVI, no. 1247 (September 26, 2006): 51.

      – "Carole M. Berotte Joseph, Ph.D.," President's Bio from Massachusetts Bay Community College, accessed January 24, 2011, http://www.massbay. edu/AboutUs/PresidentsOffice/PresidentsBio.aspx.

71   Garry Pierre-Pierre, "Dr. Carole Berotte Joseph Named President of Bronx Community College," *Haitian Times,* accessed December 29, 2011, http://haitiantimes.com/view/full_story/11122431/article-Dr—Carole-Berotte-Joseph-Named-President-of-Bronx-Community-College.

72   John H. McClendon III, "Reason, Charles Lewis (1818–1893)," from Blackpast.org, accessed December 12, 2011, http://www.blackpast.org/?q=aah/reason-charles-lewis-1818-1893.

73   Ibid.

74   Ibid.

75   Ibid.

76   Michel S. Laguerre, *American Odyssey: Haitians in New York City* (Ithaca, NY: Cornell University Press, 1984), 167.

77   Anthony W. Neal, "Boston's Black Medical Community Thrived in the Mid-19th Century," *Bay State Banner,* accessed February 25, 2013, http://www.baystatebanner.com/local13-2012-04-12.

Explorers and Settlers

78   Jacob W. Myers, "History of the Gallatin Salines," *Journal of the Illinois State Historical Society* (June 9, 2003), accessed October 14, 2007, http://www.illinoishistory.com/1922-gallatinsalines.html.

79   J. A. Rogers, *Your History: From the Beginning of Time to the Present* (Baltimore, MD: Black Classic Press, 1989), 79.

80   Carole Boyce Davies, *Encyclopedia of the African Diaspora: Origins, Experiences, and Culture* (Santa Barbara, Calif: ABC-CLIO, 2008), 403.

81   Joseph Dorsey, "du Sable, Jean-Baptiste Pointe (1745–1818)," in *Encyclopedia of the African Diaspora: Origins, Experiences and Culture*, ed. Carole Boyce-Davies (Santa Barbara, Calif: ABC-CLIO, 2007), 402–403.

82   Thelma Wills Foote, *Black and White Manhattan: The History of Racial Formation in Colonial New York City* (New York: Oxford University Press, 2004), 25.

83   James Oliver Horton and Lois E. Horton, *Slavery and the Making of America* (New York: Oxford University Press, 2004), 34.

84   Rogers, 82.

85   Jeffrey C. Stewart, *1001 Things Everyone Should Know about African American History* (New York: Gramercy Books, 2006), 3–4.

Great Families of Haitian Descent

86   Beatrice J. Fleming and Marion J. Pryde, *Distinguished Negroes Abroad* (Washington, DC: Associated Publishers, 1946), 70.

87 J. A. Rogers, *World's Great Men of Color,* volume II (New York: A Touchstone Book, 1996), 100.

88 Fleming and Pryde, 70.

89 Ibid., 72.

90 Rogers, 99.

91 Ibid., 100–101.

92 Ibid., 101.

93 Fleming and Pryde, 72.

94 Rogers, 103.
        – Fleming and Pryde, 73–74.

95 Rogers, 103.

96 Fleming and Pryde, 74–75.
        – Rogers, 104.

97 Fleming and Pryde, 75.

98 Ibid., 76.

99 Rogers, 107.

100 Fleming and Pryde, 79–80.

101 Ibid., 80–81.

102 Susannah Cahalan, "Dreams of His Father: The Surprising Inspiration Behind Alexandre Dumas' Rollicking Adventures 'The Three Musketeers' and 'Monte Cristo.'" *New York Post*, Sep. 30, 2012, accessed February 27, 2013, http://search.proquest.com/docview/1081701661?accountid=27899.

103 Ibid.

104 Rogers, 119–120.

105 Fleming and Pryde, 81–82.
        – Rogers, 119

106 Fleming and Pryde, 84.

107 Ibid., 86.

108 Pat McNamara, "Edmonia Lewis: Artist, Woman of Color, Catholic as a Black Catholic artist, Lewis brought a uniquely African perspective to her religious work," *Patheos Catholic* [Catholic Channel Section], November 1, 2010, accessed March 13, 2013, http://www.patheos.com/Resources/Additional-Resources/Edmonia-Lewis-Artist-Woman-of-Color-Catholic.html.

109 Ibid.

110 Ibid.

111 Ibid.

112 Mary Pickett, "Samuel W. Lewis: Orphan leaves mark on Bozeman," *Gazette* Staff, March 1, 2002, accessed March 13, 2013, http://billingsgazette.com/lifestyles/samuel-w-lewis-orphan-leaves-mark-on-bozeman/article_bf7abce6-bbf5-5fe2-8269-d891f9e0682a.html#ixzz2NT4NPYSA.
        – Phyllis Smith, *Bozeman and the Gallatin Valley: A History* (Helena, Montana: Falcon Press Publ., 1996), 91.

113 Pickett.
        – Smith, 91.
114 Pickett.
115 Smith, 91.
116 Ibid.

Haitian Fighting Style

117 Adam Hochschild, "Birth of a Nation: Has the Bloody 200-year History of Haiti Doomed It to More Violence?" *San Francisco Chronicle*, Sunday, May 30, 2004, accessed December 20, 2006,
        http://sfgate.com/cgibin/article.cgi?file=/chronicle/archive/2004/05/30/CMGKG6F3UV1.DTL.
118 T. J. Desch-Obi, "Peinillas and Popular Participation: Machete Fighting in Haiti, Cuba and Colombia Memorias," *Revista Digital de Historia y Arqueología desde el Caribe*, 6, núm. 11 (Noviembre-sin mes, 2009): 144–172, Universidad del Norte Colombia, 147, accessed February 28, 2013, http://redalyc.uaemex.mx/src/inicio/ArtPdfRed.jsp?iCve=85512905010.
119 Ibid., 147–148.
120 Ibid., 148.
121 Ibid., 148.
122 Ibid., 148.
123 Ibid., 148.
124 M.Desch-Obi and J. Thomas, *Fighting for Honor: The History of African Martial Art Traditions in the Atlantic World* (Columbia, SC: University of South Carolina Press, 2008), 282.
125 Thomas A. Green, *Martial Arts in the Modern World*. (Westport, CT: Praeger, 2003), 133.

Inventors

126 Mary Bellis, "Black History Month - African American Patent Holders – A:" Inventors.about, accessed December 20, 2006, http://inventors.about.com/od/photogallery/ig/African-American-Inventors---A/Marc-Auguste--7-083-512-.htm

127 The Editor, "Contemporary African-American Inventors," *Madame Noire* website dated January 10, 2011, accessed July 24, 2012, http://madamenoire.com/106958/contemporary-african-americans-inventors/.

– Herb Boyd, "Black Inventors—Past and Present," *Network Journal* website dated March 30, 2011, accessed July 24, 2012, http://www.tnj.com/news/black-american/black-inventors%E2%80%94past-and-present-0.

128 "Quebec, Canada, 28th International Conference on Digital Printing Technologies, Society for Imaging Science & Technology," Linkedin.com, accessed July 25, 2012, http://events.linkedin.com/nip-28-short-course-1053541.

– Mike F. Molaire Biography, Amazon.com (information for the biography was provided by the author or his representative), accessed July 25, 2012, http://www.amazon.com/Mike-F.-Molaire/e/B005XRWLPW.

129 Mike F. Molaire Biography.

130 Ibid.

131 Patricia Carter Sluby, *The Inventive Spirit of African Americans: Patented Ingenuity* (Westport, CT: Praeger, 2004), 104.

132 Ben Chapman, "Haitian Immigrant-filled Robotics Team Earns Contest Berth with Winning Robot," *NY Daily News*, Tuesday, March 22, 2011, accessed January 29, 2013, http://www.nydailynews.com/new-york/brooklyn/haitian-immigrant-filled-robotics-team-earns-contest-berth-winning-robot-article-1.120339.

Law and Politics

133 Patrick Sylvain, "Ertha Pascal-Trouillot: Unsung Heroine of Democracy," *Boston Haitian Reporter*, March 14, 2011, accessed January 4, 2012, http://www.bostonhaitian.com/node/411.

134 Associated Press, "Dominican-Haitian Activist Sonia Pierre Dies at 48," *Boston Haitian Reporter*, December 5, 2011, accessed December 22, 2011, http://www.bostonhaitian.com/2011/dominican-haitian-activist-sonia-pierre-dies-48.

135 Patrick Gaspard, "Haiti: One Year Later," *Whitehouse Blog*, January 12, 2011, accessed December 22, 2011, http://www.whitehouse.gov/blog/2011/01/12/haiti-one-year-later.

136 Patrick Gaspard, DiscovertheNetworks.org, accessed December 22, 2011, http://www.discoverthenetworks.org/individualProfile.asp?indid=2420.

– Domenico Montanaro, "Gaspard Named WH Political Director," *FirstRead,* MSNBC news online, Nov. 21, 2008, accessed December 2, 2008, http://firstread.msnbc.msn.com/archive/2008/11/21/1685663.aspx.

137 Patrick Gaspard, DiscovertheNetworks.org.

138 "Michaëlle Jean," The Canadian Encyclopedia, accessed February 16, 2011, http://www.thecanadianencyclopedia.com/index.cfm?PgNm=TCE&Params=A1ARTA0009825#ArticleContents.

– Famous Canadian Women's Famous Firsts, accessed February 16, 2011, http://www.famouscanadianwomen.com/famous%20firsts/politicians%20 and%20public%20servants.htm.

– Allison Cross, "In her five-year term, Michaelle Jean snacked on seal and prorogued Parliament—twice," *Gazette,* montrealgazette.com, July 8, 2010, accessed February 16, 2011, http://www.montrealgazette.com/life/five +year+term+Michaelle+Jean+snacked+seal+prorogued+Parliament+ twice/3250346/story.html.

139 "The Charming and Photogenic Michaëlle Jean (27th Governor General of Canada)," accessed February 16, 2011, http://hubpages.com /hub/The-charming-and-photogenic-Michalle-Jean-27th-Governor-General-of-Canada.

140 "Gov. Gen. Jean Gets 21-gun Salute," CBC News, September 29, 2010, accessed February 16, 2011, http://www.cbc.ca/canada/story/2010/09/29/ govenor-general-saluted-929.html.

141 "The Charming and Photogenic Michaëlle Jean (27th Governor General of Canada)."

142 Doug Mackey, "Mattawa's Dr. Firmin Monestime Remembered," *Community Voices,* (Heritage Perspectives), *October 26, 2007, accessed January 4, 2012, http://www.pastforward.ca/perspectives/columns/07_10_26.htm.*

143 "First Haitian Illinois State Senator: Haitian Immigrant's Son Kwame Raoul to replace Barack Obama in Illinois," Dec 13, 2004, accessed December 14, 2004, http://haitixchange.com/hx/article.asp?article_id=31&index=0.

– Biography, State Sen. Kwame Raoul, Illinois' 13th Legislative District, accessed December 22, 2011, http://www.kwameraoul.com/kwame_bio.html.

144 Régine Barjon, *Effectiveness of Aid in Haiti and How Private Investment Can Facilitate the Reconstruction,* written statement of Régine Barjon to the US Senate Subcommittees of Foreign Relations on International Development and Foreign Assistance and Western Hemisphere hearing entitled "Rebuilding Haiti in the Martelly Era," Thursday, June 23, 2011, accessed December 29, 2011, http://www.foreign.senate.gov/imo/media/doc/Simon-Barjon%20 testimony.pdf.

Medical

145 Rogers, *World's Great Men of Color,* vol. 2, 553.

146 "Black Woman Surgeon Saves Life of Boy, 13, with Liver Transplant," *Jet* magazine 81, no. 25 (April 13, 1992): 36–38.

147 *Haitian Historical and Cultural Legacy: A Journey Through Time A Resource Guide for Teachers,* HABETAC, 24, accessed December 29, 2011, http://*

depthome.brooklyn.cuny.edu/habetac/Publications_files/Haitian-Historical.
pdf

148 Ibid, 24.

149 Régine Barjon, *Effectiveness of Aid in Haiti and How Private Investment Can Facilitate the Reconstruction,* written statement of Régine Barjon to the US Senate Subcommittees of Foreign Relations on International Development and Foreign Assistance and Western Hemisphere hearing entitled "Rebuilding Haiti in the Martelly Era," Thursday, June 23, 2011, accessed December 29, 2011, http://www.foreign.senate.gov/imo/media/doc/Simon-Barjon%20 testimony.pdf.

Military, Revolts, Revolutions, and Wars

150 Burke Davis, *Black Heroes of the American Revolution,* foreword by Edward W. Brooke (New York: Harcourt Brace & Company, 1996), 68.

151 George P. Clark, "The Role of the Haitian Volunteers at Savannah in 1779: An Attempt at an Objective View," *Phylon (1960–)* 41, no. 4 (4th Qtr., 1980): 360.

152 Ibid., 358.

153 "French Military Units," *W3R [Washington-Rochambeau Revolutionary Route],* accessed March 22, 2013, http://www.w3r-us.org/history/milu-fr.htm.

154 Ibid.

155 Philippe R. Girard, *Haiti: The Tumultuous History—From Pearl of the Caribbean to Broken Nation* (New York: Palgrave Macmillan, 2010), 74.

156 Ibid., 54.

157 Alice Morse Earle, *Stage-coach and Tavern Days* (New York: Macmillan Co., 1900), 183.

158 Charles L. Blockson, "Black Samuel Fraunces Patriot, White House Steward and Restaurateur Par Excellence," Temple University Libraries website, accessed February 16, 2012, http://library.temple.edu/collections/blockson/fraunces. jsp;jsessionid=284E5B2DB0413B6C2DEC05D1D0778B5E?bhcp=1.

159 "Fraunces Tavern," MAAP produced by the Columbia Center for New Media Teaching and Learning (CCNMTL) in partnership with Columbia University's Teachers College and Creative Curriculum Initiatives (CCI), accessed February 16, 2012, http://maap.columbia.edu/place/3.html.

160 Blockson.

161 "Fraunces Tavern," MAAP.
     – Blockson.

162 "Fraunces Tavern," MAAP.

163 Earle, 184.

164 Blockson.

165 "Fraunces Tavern," MAAP.
   – Blockson.

166 Blockson.

167 "Fraunces Tavern Historical Landmark," Historical Makers from ExplorePAhistory.com, accessed February 16, 2012, http://explorepahistory. com/hmarker.php?markerId=1-A-28A.
   – Blockson.

168 Stephan Salisbury, "At Last, Honoring the Burial Site of 'Black Sam'," Philly.com, June 25, 2010, accessed February 16, 2012, http://articles.philly. com/2010-06-25/news/24966504_1_burial-site-racial-identity-descendants.

169 Blockson.

170 Salisbury.

171 Ibid.

172 Ibid.

173 "Honoring Samuel Fraunces at St. Peter's, June 26, 2010," The President's House in Philadelphia, accessed February 16, 2012, http://www.ushistory.org/ presidentshouse/history/frauncesobelisk.htm.

174 "Haitian Immigration: Eighteenth and Nineteenth Centuries," Schomburg Center for Research in Black Culture, the New York Public Library, accessed February 27, 2013, http://www.inmotionaame.org/print. cfm;jsessionid=f830178511361544584816?migration=5&bhcp=1.
   – Nancy Cho, "Savary, Joseph (?–1800's)," Blackpast.org, accessed February 27, 2013, http://www.blackpast.org/?q=aah/savary-joseph.

175 "Haitian Immigration: Eighteenth and Nineteenth Centuries," Schomburg Center for Research in Black Culture, the New York Public Library.

176 "Best of the Blogs," Savannah Morning News, Jan. 11, 2007, accessed February 5, 2013, http://search.proquest.com/docview/381895735?accountid=14375.

177 B. Francone, "Service of Family Member Makes National History: Grave Marker Honors Haitian-American's Participation in Civil War," Savannah Morning News, Nov. 12, 2007, accessed February 5, 2013, http://search. proquest.com/docview/381955130?accountid=27899.

178 Melissa Daggett, "Henry Louise Rey, Spiritualism, and Creoles of Color in Nineteenth-Century New Orleans," University of New Orleans Theses and Dissertations. Paper 994, 2009, 3, accessed February 21, 2013, http:// scholarworks.uno.edu/cgi/viewcontent.cgi?article=1975&context=td.

179 Lawrence L. Hewitt and Arthur W. Bergeron, *Louisianians in the Civil War* (Columbia: University of Missouri Press, 2002), 106, accessed February 21, 2013, http://search.ebscohost.com/login.aspx?direct=true&scope=site&db=nlebk& db=nlabk&AN=113912.

180 Dr. Claud Anderson and Brant Anderson, *More Dirty Little Secrets About Black History, Its Heroes, and Other Troublemakers,* vol. 2 (Maryland: PowerNomics Corporation of America, 2006), 29.

– John E. Worth, "History and Archaeology: Spanish Exploration," *The New Georgia Encyclopedia*, Oct. 17, 2003, accessed January 9, 2008, http://www.georgiaencyclopedia.org/nge/Article.jsp?id=h-1012.

– Herbert Aptheker, *American Negro Slave Revolts* (New York: Columbia University Press, 1943), 163.

181 Aptheker, 163.

– Anderson and Anderson, 29.

– Woodbury Lowery, *The Spanish Settlements Within the Present Limits of the United States, 1513–1561* (New York: Russell & Russell, Inc., 1959), 167.

– Justin Winsor, *Narrative and Critical History of America,* vol. 2 (Boston, New York: Houghton, Mifflin and Company, 1886), 241.

182 Aptheker, 163.

183 R. R. Wright, "Negro Companions of the Spanish Explorers," *American Anthropologist*, New Series, vol. 4, no. 2 (April–June 1902): 217–228. (This event can be found on pp. 220–221).

– Anderson and Anderson, 29–30.

– Aptheker, 163.

184 Wright, 221.

185 Anderson and Anderson, 30.

– Aptheker, 163.

– Lowery, 167–168.

– Winsor, 241.

186 Anderson and Anderson, 30.

187 Ibid., 30.

188 Wright, 221.

189 Lerone Bennett Jr., *Before the Mayflower: A History of the Negro in America 1619–1962* (Chicago: Johnson Publishing Company, Inc. 1962), 101.

190 Anderson and Anderson, 31.

191 Aylmer Von Fleischer, *Retake Your Fame: Black Contribution to World Civilization* (Bloomington, Indiana: Authorhouse, 2004), 88.

192 J. A. Rogers, *100 Amazing Facts About The Negro With Complete Proof* (New York: H. M. Rogers, 1995), 21.

193 J. A. Rogers, *World's Great Men of Color,* vol. 2 (New York: A Touchstone Book, 1996), 74–75.

194 Ibid., 75.

195 Ibid., 75–76.

196 Ibid., 76.

197 J. A. Rogers, *Sex and Race, Volume 2: The New World* (United States, 1967), 150.

198 Gail Lumet Buckley, *American Patriots: The Story of Blacks in the Military from the Revolution to Desert Storm* (New York, NY: Random House, 2002).

199 Evan Andrews, "7 Famous Slaves Revolts," A&E Television Networks [History], accessed January 29, 2013, http://www.history.com/news/history-lists/7-famous-slave-revolts.

200 Robert Debs Heinl and Nancy Gordon Heinl, *Written in Blood* (Lanham: University Press of America, 2005), 18.

– Jacques Nicolas Leger, *Haiti, Her History and Her Detractors* (Westport, Connecticut: Negro Universities Press, 1970), 34.

–*A Biographical Dictionary of the Flibuste (1648–1688)*, accessed December 3, 2006, http://translate.google.com/translate?hl=en&sl=fr&u=http://www.oricom.ca/yarl/PQ/P.html&sa=X&oi=translate&resnum=3&ct=result&prev=/search%3Fq%3DPadrejean%2B%26hl%3Den%26lr%3D%26safe%3Doff%26rls%3DGGLD,GGLD:2003-47,GGLD:en.

– A. J. Victor, *In the Name of Liberty: A History of Haiti (Pre-1492–1806)* (Linivè Kreyòl, 2004), 82.

201 Heinl and Heinl, 18.

– Perusse, 78.

– Leger, 34.

– Victor, 82.

202 Rogers, *100 Amazing Facts,* 20.

203 Ibid., 46.

204 Ibid., 20.

205 Andrew Frank, *The Birth of Black America: The Age of Discovery and The Slave Trade* (New York: Chelsea House Publishers, 1996), 107.

206 Thomas and Dorothy Hoobler, *Toussaint Louverture* (New York: Chelsea House Publishers, 1990), 98–99.

– Carolyn E.Fick, *The Making of Haiti: The Saint Domingue Revolution from Below* (Knoxville: The University of Tennessee Press, 1990), 229.

207 C. L. R. James, *The Black Jacobins: Toussaint Louverture and The San Domingo Revolution* (New York: Vintage Books, 1989), 358.

208 Adam Hochschild, "Birth of a Nation: Has the Bloody 200-year History of Haiti Doomed It to More Violence?" *San Francisco Chronicle*, Sunday, May 30, 2004, accessed December 20, 2006, http://sfgate.com/cgibin/article.cgi?file=/chronicle/archive/2004/05/30/CMGKG6F3UV1.DTL.

– Robert Lawless, *Haiti's Bad Press*, (Rochester, Vermont: Schenkman Books, Inc., 1992), 43.

209 Victor, 195.

210 Victor, 194.

– James, 359

211 James, 359.

212 Randle Robinson, *An Unbroken Agony: Haiti, From Revolution to the Kidnapping of a President* (New York: A Member of the Perseus Books Group, 2007), 13.

213 Victor, 195.

214 Joan Dayan, *Haiti, History, and the Gods* (Berkeley: University of California Press, 1995), 155.

– Victor, 195.

215 Victor, 195.

216 Ibid., 197.

217 Ibid.

218 Dayan, 155.

– Martin Ros, *Night of Fire: The Black Napoleon and the Battle for Haiti* (United States: Da Capo Press, 1994), 194.

219 Victor, 202.

220 Laurent Dubois, *Avengers of the New World: The Story of the Haitian Revolution* (Cambridge, Massachusetts: Harvard University Press, 2004), 293.

– Victor, 202.

221 James, 359.

222 Hoobler, Thomas, and Dorothy, 102.

223 James, 361.

224 Bennett, 109.

225 Hudson, Christopher. "The French Fuhrer: Genocidal Napoleon was as Barbaric as Hitler, Historian Claims," *Daily Mail*, July 24, 2008. (Accessed March 12, 2012).

http://www.dailymail.co.uk/news/article-1038453/The-French-Fuhrer-Genocidal-Napoleon-barbaric-Hitler-historian-claims.html#ixzz2McmaOv1T.

226 Ibid.

227 Dubois, *Avengers of the New World,* 110.

228 Ibid.

229 Ibid.

230 Ibid.

231 Hochschild.

232 Ibid.

233 David Geggus, "The British Government and The Saint Domingue Slave Revolt, 1791–1793," *English Historical Review* 96, no. 379 (April 1981): 285–305.

234 Richards Watts, "Dessalines, Jean-Jacques" in *Africana: The Encyclopedia of the African and African American Experience*, second edition, vol. 2, Catimbó–Giovanni (Oxford University Press, 2005), 368.

235 John Relly Beard, *The Life of Toussaint Louverture the Negro Patriot of Hayti: Comprising an Account of the Struggle for Liberty in the Island, and a Sketch of Its History to the Present Period* (London: Ingram, Cooke, and Co., 1853), 194.

236 James, 361–362.

237 Fick, 221.

238 Jayne Boisvert, "Colonial Hell and Female Resistance in Saint-Domingue," *Journal of Haitian Studies* 7, no. 1 (spring 2001): 73.

239 Ibid.

240 Catherine Reinhardt, "Heroine Maroon Slave," in *Revolutionary Freedoms: A History of Survival, Strength and Imagination in Haiti* (Caribbean Studies Press, Imprint of Educa Vision Inc., 2006), 79.

241 Ibid.

242 Bernard Moitt, *Women and Slavery in the French Antilles, 1635–1848* (Indiana University Press, 2001), 128.

243 Ibid.,129.

244 Laurent Dubois, *Avengers of the New World: The Story of the Haitian Revolution* (Cambridge, Massachusetts: Harvard University Press, 2004), 295.

245 Moitt, 144.

246 Ibid., 127–128.

247 Margaret Mitchell Armand, "Marie-Jeanne Lamartinierre," in *Revolutionary Freedoms: A History of Survival, Strength and Imagination in Haiti* (Caribbean Studies Press, Imprint of Educa Vision Inc., 2006), 85–86.

248 Boisvert, 73.

249 Georges Jean-Charles, *Dictionnaire Historique de la Révolution Haïtienne (1789–1804)*, (Montréal, Québec: Éditions Images; Éditions du CIDIHCA, 2003), 51.

250 DiscoverHaiti: "Jean-Jacques Dessalines: 1758–1806, Hero or Tyrant? Part 1," *History*, accessed May 14, 2008, http://www.discoverhaiti.com/history00_10_1.htm.

251 François Roc, *Dictionnaire de la Révolution Haïtienne, 1789-1804: Dictionnaire des Evénements, des Emblèmes et Devises, des Institutions et Actes, des Leux et des Personnages* (Montréal: Éditions Guildives, 2006), 361.

    – Femmes d'Haiti, 2005: "Henriett Saint-Marc," Femme Célèbres, accessed May 14, 2008, http://www.haiticulture.ch/.

252 Vistor, 223.

253 Fick, 265.

254 Ibid., 104.

255 Ibid., 266.

256 Ibid., 266.

257 Ibid., 242.

258 Nicole Jean-Louis, *History and Culture of Haiti: Journey Through Visual Art* (Xlibris Corporation, 2012).

259 Robinson, 11.

260 William Leslie Balan-Gaubert, "A Great Moment in Haitian History," Nov. 5, 2004, accessed April 24, 2008, http://www.ahadonline.org/eLibrary/creoleconnection/Number16/greatmoment.htm.

    – W. F. Burton Sellers, "Heroes of Haiti," January 11, 1999, accessed April 24, 2008, http://www.hartford-hwp.com/archives/43a/168.html.

261 Balan-Gaubert.

262 Sellers.

    – Balan-Gaubert.

    – Robinson, 11.

    – Victor, 207.

263 Balan-Gaubert.

264 Robinson, 11.

265 Nigel Jones, "The Black Count: Glory, Revolution, Betrayal and the Real Count of Monte Cristo by Tom Reiss—review," *Guardian*, Friday, September 28, 2012, accessed February 27, 2013, http://www.guardian.co.uk/books/2012/sep/28/black-count-tom-reiss-review.

266 James W. Loewen, *Lies My Teacher Told Me: Everything Your American History Textbook Got Wrong* (New York: New Press, 2008), 150, accessed May 14, 2010, http://public.eblib.com/EBLPublic/PublicView.do?ptiID=579047.

267 Cécile Accilien, Jessica Adams, Elmide Méléance, and Jean-Pierre Ulrick, *Revolutionary Freedoms* (Coconut Creek, FL: Caribbean Studies Press, 2006), 122.

268 Ibid.

269 Spencer Tucker, *A Global Chronology of Conflict: From the Ancient World to the Modern Middle East* (Santa Barbara, CA: ABC-CLIO, 2010), 1405.

270 Ibid.

271 Nancy Cho, "Savary, Joseph (?–1800s)," Blackpast.org., accessed February 27, 2013, http://www.blackpast.org/?q=aah/savary-joseph.

    – "Haitian Immigration: Eighteenth and Nineteenth Centuries," Schomburg Center for Research in Black Culture, the New York Public Library.

272 Harry Hamilton Johnston, *The Negro in the New World* (London: Macmillan, 1910), 48.

273 Teresa A. Meade, *A History of Modern Latin America, 1800–2000* (Oxford: Blackwell, 2008), 75.

274 Buckley, 169.

275 "Eugene Jacques Bullard," National Museum of the USAF, accessed February 16, 2011, http://www.nationalmuseum.af.mil/factsheets/factsheet.asp?id=705.

276 Carla W. Garner, "Bullard, Eugene Jacques (1894–1961)," from Blackpast.com, accessed February 16, 2011, http://www.blackpast.org/?q=aah/bullard-eugene-jacques-1894-1961.

277 Ibid.

278 Buckley, 169.

279 "Eugene Jacques Bullard," National Museum of the USAF.

280 Fleurimond W. Kerns, "The Haitian Flag—Birth of a Symbol," trans. Greg Dunkel, May 18, 2003, from International Action Center, accessed January 6, 2012, http://www.iacenter.org/haiti/flag.htm.

   – Greg Dunkel, "Haitian History: What U.S. Textbooks Don't Tell," *Haiti Progress, This Week in Haiti* 21, no. 27 (September 2003): 17–23, accessed January 6, 2012, http://www.hartford-hwp.com/archives/43a/549.html.

   – Edna Taft, *A Puritan in Voodoo-Land* (Philadelphia: Penn Pub. Co., 1938), 157–158.

281 Kerns.

   – Dunkel.

   – Taft, 158.

282 "Haiti History 101," *The Haitian Tuskegee Airmen,* accessed July 24, 2012, http://kreyolicious.com/haiti-history-101-the-haitian-tuskegee-airmen/1597/.

   – "Tuskegee Airmen Pilot Listing," *Tuskegee University,* accessed July 24, 2012, http://kreyolicious.com/haiti-history-101-the-haitian-tuskegee-airmen/1597/.

283 "Haiti History 101."

   – "Always Remembering His Dad—A Tuskegee Airman," accessed July 24, 2012, http://www.broward.org/ECountyLine/Pages/Vol_36_no_5/mainStory1.htm.

284 "Haiti History 101."

   – "Raymond Cassagnol," fordi9.com, accessed July 24, 2012, http://www.fordi9.com/Pages/AffairCassagnol.htm).

285 "Haiti History 101."

286 Ibid.

287 Ibid.

288 Ibid.

289 "Tuskegee Airmen Pilot Listing," *Tuskegee University.*

290 Anne Lies, *The Earthquake in Haiti* (Edina, Minnesota: ABDO Pub., 2001), 32.

291 Johnston, 48.

292 Ha'aretz Nirit Ben-Ari, "Haiti and the Jews: Forgotten History," Translation: Pacha Dovinsky, from *World War 4 Report*, February 1, 2010 [Nirit Ben-Ari is a doctoral student in political science who teaches at Israel's Sapir College. This article first appeared in Hebrew in the Israeli daily *Ha'aretz* on Jan. 22], accessed January 4, 2012, http://ww4report.com/node/8272.

293 "The Virtual Jewish History Tour Haiti," Jewish Virtual Library, accessed January 3, 2012, http://www.jewishvirtuallibrary.org/jsource/vjw/haiti.html.

294 Nirit Ben-Ari.

Miscellaneous

295 Frederick J. Simonelli, *The Historical Encyclopedia of World Slavery,* vol. 1, A–K (Santa Barbara, CA: ABC-CLIO, 1997), 325.

296 Joseph Willson and Julie Winch, *The Elite of Our People: Joseph Willson's Sketches of Black Upper-Class Life in Antebellum Philadelphia* (University Park: Pennsylvania State University Press, 2000), 123.
– George E. Stephens and Donald Yacovone, *A Voice of Thunder: A Black Soldier's Civil War* (Urbana: University of Illinois Press, 1998), 185.

297 Willson and Winch, 158.

298 Ibid., 123.

299 Mark Pygas, "10 Amazing Female Pirates," Listverse, 2013, http://listverse. com/2013/09/28/10-amazing-female-pirates/.

300 Charles H. Parker, *Global Interactions in the Early Modern Age 1400-1800* (Leiden: Cambridge University Press, 2010), 77.

301 Mark Pygas.

302 Jaclyn (Yellow Sea), "Who's not captivated by a woman known as 'Back from the Dead Red'?." 2013, https://3sistersofsea.wordpress.com/2013/06/08/ whos-not-captivated-by-a-woman-known-as-back-from-the-dead-red/.

303 "Lincoln Poems," Millikin University, accessed December 10, 2008, https:// www.millikin.edu/english/Guillory'sWeb/www/Lincolnpoems.html.

304 "Lincoln Poems," Millikin University; James Krohe, *Honest Abe's Honest Almanac: Being a Cornucopia of Amazing Facts, Useful Wisdom, and Amusing Anecdotes Concerning the Social, Political, Economic, Recreational, Educational, and Cultural Life of Springfield, Illinois, Past and Present* (Springfield, Ill: Talisman Press, 1974), 8, accessed December 10, 2008, http://www.archive.org/details/honestabeshonest00kroh.

305 Ibid.

306 "Lincoln Poems," Millikin University; Kathryn M. Harris, "Generations of Pride: African American Timeline: A Selected Chronology," Illinois Historic Preservation Agency from the Abraham Lincoln Presidential Library, accessed December 10, 2008, http://www.illinoishistory.gov/lib/ GenPrideAfAm.htm.

307 Ibid.

308 Ruth Cobb, *History & Mystery: Wall Art in Downtown Bloomington* (*Who are these people, and why are they on the wall?*), b-n.com, accessed December 10, 2008, http://www.b-n.com/pages/bsWallArtdwtnBlm.html.

309 John A.Williams, "Edmond Family's Secret Turns Out to Be Revealing Story," *Newsok* website, November 8, 2008, accessed December 10, 2008, http://newsok.com/edmond-familys-secret-turns-out-to-be-revealing-story/ article/3319937.

310 Karlson Yu, "Springfield Race Riot, 1908," BlackPast.org, accessed December 10, 2008, http://www.blackpast.org/?q=aah/springfield-race-riot-1908.

311 Zondra Hughes, "What Happened to the Only Black Family on the Titanic," *Ebony* LV, no. 8 (June 2000): 148–150.

312 Ibid., 150.

313 Ibid., 152.

314 Ibid., 154.

315 Cécile Accilien, Jessica Adams, Elmide Méléance, and Jean-Pierre Ulrick, *Revolutionary Freedoms* (Coconut Creek, FL: Caribbean Studies Press, 2006), 126.

316 "Timeless designs by Berny Martin," *Beyond Africa* magazine, accessed May 24, 2015, http://www.beyondafricamagazine.com/?p=326.
      – NAHP, "Berny Martin," accessed May 24, 2015, http://nahpusa.org/berny-martin/.

317 J. A. Rogers, *Sex and Race, Volume 2: The New World* (United States, 1967), 104.

318 Nicole Jean-Louis, *History and Culture of Haiti: Journey Through Visual Art* (Xlibris Corporation, 2012).

319 Erica Pearson, "It's Supergirl!" *New York Daily News* newspaper, Sunday, May 15, 2011, 22.

Pilots

320 Lawrence P. Scott and William M. Womack, *Double V: The Civil Rights Struggle of the Tuskegee Airmen* (East Lansing, MI: Michigan State University Press, 1998), 35, accessed July 24, 2012, http://search.ebscohost.com/login.aspx?direct=true&scope=site&db=nlebk&db=nlabk&AN=22823.

321 "Charles Terres Weymann, 1889–1976, AKA Charles II Weymann," accessed July 24, 2012, http://earlyaviators.com/eweymann.htm.

322 Economic Times, accessed July 31, 2012, http://economictimes.indiatimes.com/topic/Charles-Terres-Weymann/photos.

323 *Automobile Topics*, New York, July 8, 1911, vol. XXII, no. 14 (Detroit, MI: Ward's Automobile Topics), 701.

324 "Weymann-American Body Company, 1926–1932; Indianapolis, Indiana," Coachbuilt, accessed July 31, 2012, http://www.coachbuilt.com/bui/w/weymann/weymann.htm.
      – "Bugatti," Mini.43, accessed July 31, 2012, http://mini.43.free.fr/bugattiroyales.html.

Production

325 André Juste, "Haiti," in *Africana: The Encyclopedia of the African and African American Experience* (New York: Basic Civitas Books, 2005), 116.

– Laurent Dubois and John D. Garrigus, *Slave Revolution in the Caribbean, 1789–1804: A Brief History with Documents* (Boston, MA; New York, NY: Bedford/St. Martins, 2006), 11.

– John Garrigus, "Haiti Independence Revolution," in *Revolutionary Movement in World History From 1750 to the Present,* vol. 2, H–P (Santa Barbara, California: ABC CLIO, 2006), 359.

326 Mary C. Truck, *Haiti: Land of Inequality* (Minneapolis: Lerner Publication Company, 1999), 35.

327 Selden Rodman, *Haiti the Black Republic: The Standard Guide to Haiti* (Old Greenwich: Devin-Adair, Publishers, 1984), 8.

328 Robert Debs Heinl and Nancy Gordon Heinl, *Written in Blood* (Lanham: University Press of America, 2005), 29.

329 Martin Ros, *Night of Fire: The Black Napoleon and the Battle for Haiti* (United States: Da Capo Press, 1994), 12.

330 "Made in Haiti: Social Entrepreneurs Get a Boost," Pan American Development Foundation, February 16, 2015, http://www.padf.org/blog-hidden/2015/3/2/made-in-haiti-social-entrepreneurs-get-a-boost.

331 Daniella Bien-Aime, "4 Emerging Startups of Haitian Influence You Should Know," *Haitian Times*, March 30, 2015, http://haitiantimes.com/4-emerging-startups-of-haitian-influence-you-should-know-10917/.

332 Alfred Edmond Jr., "UBR Spotlight: Meet Successful Teen CEO Leanna Archer," Black Enterprise, accessed January 29, 2013, http://www.blackenterprise.com/small-business/ubr-spotlight-meet-successful-teen-ceo-leanna-archer/.

– "Profile: Leanna Archer, Fouunder and CEO of Leanna's Inc," The Habari Network, accessed January 29, 2013, http://www.thehabarinetwork.com/profile-leanna-archer-founder-and-ceo-of-leanna%E2%80%99s-inc.

333 Dina Evans, "Barbancourt," Webster University home page of Bob Corbett, accessed February 15, 2011, http://www.webster.edu/~corbetre/haiti/misctopic/leftover/rhum.htm.

334 Rhum Barbancourt, accessed February 15, 2011, http://www.barbancourt.net/index2.php?mode=1&langue=en.

335 "Reserve," Rhum Barbancourt, accessed February 15, 2011, http://www.barbancourt.net/rhum-barbancourt-reserve-du-domaine.php?langue=en.

336 Brewers Association Presents World Beer Cup 2000 Winner List, accessed on February 15, 2011, http://www.worldbeercup.org/pdf/2000_winners.pdf.

Religion

337 "The Haitian Influence on Religion," In Motion: The African-American Migration Experience, accessed October 20, 2006, http://www.inmotionaame.org/migrations/topic_body.cfm?migration=5&topic=7.

– Jone Johnson Lewis, "Henriette Delille," Women's History, About.com, accessed October 20, 2006, http://womenshistory.about.com/od/romancatholicchurch/p/h_delille.htm.

338 "The Haitian Influence on Religion."

339 Lewis.

– Franciscan University of Steubenville, accessed October 20, 2006, http://www.bcimall.org/calendar/franuniv/henriette_delille.htm.

340 "Events," Chronology of Church History, St. Augustine Catholic Church of New Orleans, accessed October 20, 2006, http://www.staugustinecatholicchurch-neworleans.org/hist-chron.htm.

341 "Elizabeth Clarisse Lange (aka Mother Mary)," Other Great Blacks, Black Catholics, accessed October 19, 2006, http://www.nbccongress.org/black-catholics/elizabeth-clarisse-lange-famous-blacks.asp.

– "Mother Mary Elizabeth Lange," OSP, accessed October 19, 2006, http://www.oblatesisters.com/page20.html.

342 "Elizabeth Clarisse Lange (aka Mother Mary)."

– Susan Brinkmann, "Celebrating Black History Month: Relying on Providence: Mother Mary Elizabeth Lange," accessed October 19, 2006, http://www.cst-phl.com/060223/blackcatholic.html.

343 Ibid.

344 Donald R. McClarey, "Venerable Pierre Toussaint," *The American Catholic*, accessed February 15, 2013, http://the-american-catholic.com/2010/05/21/venerable-pierre-toussaint/.

345 "Pierre Toussaint," MAAP (Mapping the African American Past), accessed February 15, 2013, http://maap.columbia.edu/place/13.html.

346 "Venerable Pierre Toussaint," Archdiocese of New York, accessed February 15, 2013, http://www.obmny.org/VenerablePT.htm.

347 "Pierre Toussaint," MAAP.

348 "Venerable Pierre Toussaint," Archdiocese of New York.

349 Sisters, Servants of the Immaculate Heart of Mary, "Mother Theresa Maxis Duchemin," IHM Founder, accessed October 23, 2006, http://www.ihmimmaculata.org/history/founder.html.

– "Mother Theresa Maxis Duchemin," Maxis Foundation, Marian Community Hospital, accessed October 23, 2006, http://www.marianhospital.org/services/maxis.php.

350 "The Haitian Influence on Religion."

351 Mary Bernard Deggs, Virginia Meacham Gould, Charles E. Nolan, *No Cross, No Crown: Black Nuns in Nineteenth-Century New Orleans* (Bloomington: Indiana University Press, 2001), xxx.

352 "The Haitian Influence on Religion."
    – Lewis.

353 Deggs, Gould, Nolan, 26.

354 Ibid., 132.

355 "Events," Chronology of Church History.

356 David M. Cheney, "Bishop Guy A. Sansaricq Auxiliary Bishop Emeritus of Brooklyn, New York, Titular Bishop of Glenndálocha," *Catholic Hierarchy*, accessed February 15, 2013, http://www.catholic-hierarchy.org/bishop/bsansg.html.

357 Carolyn E. Fick, *The Making of Haiti The Saint Domingue Revolution From Below* (Knoxville: University of Tennessee Press, 1990), 73.

358 Paulette Poujol-Oriol, "Boukman," in *Africana: The Encyclopedia of the African and African American Experience*, second edition (Oxford University Press, 2005), 591.

359 Cécile Fatiman, *The Louverture Project*, accessed February 12, 2006, http://www.thelouvertureproject.org/wiki/index.php?title=C%C3%A9cile_Fatiman.

360 Ibid.

361 Martin Ros, *Night of Fire the Black Napoleon and the Battle for Haiti* (United States: Da Capo Press, 1994), 4.

362 Mary C. Truck, *Haiti Land of Inequality* (Minneapolis: Lerner Publication Company, 1999), 40.
    – Adam Hochschild, "Birth of a Nation Has the bloody 200-year history of Haiti doomed it to more violence?" *San Francisco Chronicle*, Sunday, May 30, 2004, accessed December 20, 2006, http://sfgate.com/cgibin/article.cgi?file=/chronicle/archive/2004/05/30/CMGKG6F3UV1.DTL

363 Fick, 99.

364 Robert Debs Heinl and Nancy Gordon Heinl, *Written in Blood* (Lanham: University Press of America, 2005), 39–40.

365 Ibid., 38–39.

366 Ibid., 40.

367 Ibid.

368 William Claypole and John Robottom, *Caribbean Story Book One: Foundations* (Jamaica: Carlong Publishers, 1980), 144.

369 Ros, 5.

370 Cécile Fatiman, *The Louverture Project*.

371 Fick, 265.

372 Colin Dayan, *Haiti, History, and the Gods* (Berkeley: University of California Press, 1995), 45.

373 Leon D. Pamphile, *Haitians and African Americans* (Gainesville: University Press of Florida, 2001), 63, accessed March 7, 2013, http://public.eblib.com/EBLPublic/PublicView.do?ptiID=290214.

Scholars and Writers

374 J. A. Rogers, *Your History: From the Beginning of Time to the Present* (Baltimore, MD: Black Classic Press, 1989), 52.

375 Bob Corbett, "Notes on Joseph-Antenor Firmin," Webster University, accessed January 4, 2012, http://www.webster.edu/~corbetre/haiti/history/1844-1915/firmin.htm.

376 Manolia Charlotin, "Anténor Firmin's Work Resonates at NAACP Centennial," *Boston Haitian Reporter*, October 12, 2011, accessed January 4, 2012, http://www.bostonhaitian.com/node/621.

377 Ibid.

378 Carolyn Fluehr-Lobban, "Antenor Firmin Predicted America's First Black President in 1885!" *University of Illinois Press,* January 23, 2009, accessed January 4, 2012, http://www.press.uillinois.edu/wordpress/?p=2136.

379 Ibid.

380 Ibid.

381 Elisabeth Bouvet, "Dany Laferriere, 2009 Prix Médicis," rfi.fr, accessed January 4, 2012, http://www.rfi.fr/contenu/20091104-dany-laferriere-prix-medicis-2009.
　　－ "Haitian-Born Laferriere, the First Canadian Writer to Win France's Prestigious Medicis Literary Prize," November 4, 2009, accessed January 4, 2012, http://www.wehaitians.com/dany%20laferriere%20wins%20medcis%20literary%20prize.html.

382 J. A. Rogers, *World's Great Men of Color,* vol. 2 (New York: A Touchstone Book, 1996), 553.
　　－ Victor Séjour and Norman R. Shapiro, *The Fortune-teller* (Urbana: University of Illinois Press, 2002), xv–xvi.

383 Rogers, *World's Great Men of Color,* vol. 2, 553.

Appendix

Bob Corbett, "Heads of States of Haiti: Presidents, King and Emperors," Haiti Section, accessed April 23, 2015, http://www2.webster.edu/~corbetre/haiti/misctopic/leftover/headstate.htm.

Michael R. Hall, *Historical Dictionary of Haiti* (Lanham: Scarecrow Press, 2012).

Roland I. Perusse, *Historical Dictionary of Haiti* (Metuchen, NJ: Scarecrow Press, Inc., 1977).

"Counttried and Territories (H)," Rulers.org, accessed April 23, 2015, http://rulers.org/index.html.

Quotes

"The child of a tiger is a tiger."

"Haitian Proverbs, Quotes, Quotations, and Sayings," World of Quotes, accessed June 16, 2015, http://www.worldofquotes.com/proverb/Haitian/1/%22.

"The pencil of God has no eraser."

"Proverb Quotes," Worlds of Quotes, accessed June 16, 2015, http://www.worldofquotes.com/author/Proverb/1/index.html.

"To my people" in the words of Joseph Auguste Anténor

Carolyn Fluehr-Lobban, "Antenor Firmin Predicted America's First Black President in 1885!" *University of Illinois Press,* January 23, 2009, accessed January 4, 2012, http://www.press.uillinois.edu/wordpress/?p=2136.

Bibliography

Accilien, Cécile, Jessica Adams, Elmide Méléance, and Jean-Pierre Ulrick. *Revolutionary Freedoms*. Coconut Creek, FL: Caribbean Studies Press, 2006.

"Always Remembering His Dad—A Tuskegee Airman." Accessed July 24, 2012. http://www.broward.org/ECountyLine/Pages/Vol_36_no_5/mainStory1.htm.

Anderson, Dr. Claud, and Brant Anderson. *More Dirty Little Secrets About Black History, Its Heroes, and Other Troublemakers,* vol. 2. Maryland: PowerNomics Corporation of America, 2006.

Andrews, Evan. "7 Famous Slaves Revolts." A&E Television Networks [History]. Accessed January 29, 2013. http://www.history.com/news/history-lists/7-famous-slave-revolts.

Appiah, Anthony, and Henry Louis Gates. *Africana: The Encyclopedia of the African and African American Experience*, vol. 3, 2nd ed. New York: Basic Civitas Books, 2005.

Appiah, Anthony, and Henry Louis Gates. *Africana: The Encyclopedia of the African American Experience: The Concise Desk Reference*. Philadelphia: Running Press, 2003.

Aptheker, Herbert. *American Negro Slave Revolts*. New York: Columbia University Press, 1943.

Archdiocese of New York. "Venerable Pierre Toussaint." Accessed February 15, 2013. http://www.obmny.org/VenerablePT.htm.

Armand, Margaret Mitchell. "Marie-Jeanne Lamartinierre," in *Revolutionary Freedoms: A History of Survival, Strength and Imagination in Haiti*. Caribbean Studies Press, Imprint of Educa vision Inc., 2006.

Associated Press. "African Burial Ground opens in Manhattan: Dedication ceremony comes 16 years after bones were rediscovered." MSNBC.com. Accessed October 12, 2007. http://www.msnbc.msn.com/id/21150548/.

Automobile Topics, New York. Vol. XXII, no.14 (July 8, 1911): 701.

Balan-Gaubert, William Leslie. "A Great Moment in Haitian History." (Nov. 5, 2004). Accessed April 24, 2008. http://www.ahadonline. org/eLibrary/creoleconnection/Number16/greatmoment.htm.

Barjon, Régine. *Effectiveness of Aid in Haiti and How Private Investment Can Facilitate the Reconstruction.* Written statement of Régine Barjon to the US Senate Subcommittees of Foreign Relations on International Development and Foreign Assistance and Western Hemisphere hearing entitled "Rebuilding Haiti in the Martelly Era" Thursday, June 23, 2011. Accessed December 29, 2011. http://www.foreign.senate.gov/imo/media/doc/Simon-Barjon%20testimony.pdf

Beard, John Relly. *The Life of Toussaint Louverture the Negro Patriot of Hayti: Comprising an Account of the Struggle for Liberty in the Island, and a Sketch of Its History to the Present Period.* London. Ingram, Cooke, and Co., 1853.

Bennett Jr., Lerone. *Before the Mayflower: A History of the Negro in America 1619–1962.* Chicago: Johnson Publishing Company, Inc., 1962.

Bergman, Carol. *Sidney Poitier.* Los Angeles, CA: Melrose Square Pub., 1990.

"Best of the Blogs." *Savannah Morning News.* Jan. 11, 2007. Accessed February 5, 2013. http://search.proquest.com/docview/381895735?accountid=14375.

A Biographical Dictionary of the Flibuste (1648–1688). Accessed December 3, 2006. http://translate.google.com/translate?hl=en&sl=fr&u=http://www.oricom.ca/yarl/PQ/P.html&sa=X&oi=translate&resnum=3&ct=result&prev=/search%3Fq%3DPadrejean%2B%26hl%3Den%26lr%3D%26safe%3Doff%26rls%3DGGLD,GGLD:2003-47,GGLD:en

Biography State Sen. Kwame Raoul, Illinois' 13th Legislative District. Accessed December 22, 2011. http://www.kwameraoul.com/kwame_bio.html.

The Black Archives of Mid-America in Kansas City. Accessed April 3, 2013. http://www.blackarchives.org/articles/african-americans-missouri.

Black Catholics: "Elizabeth Clarisse Lange (aka Mother Mary)," *Other Great Blacks.* Accessed October 19, 2006. http://www.nbccongress.org/black-catholics/elizabeth-clarisse-lange-famous-blacks.asp.

"Black Woman Surgeon Saves Life of Boy, 13, with Liver Transplant." *Jet* 81, no. 25 (April 13, 1992): 36–38.

"Blacks during the Holocaust." United States Holocaust Memorial Museum. Accessed January 3, 2012. http://www.ushmm.org/wlc/en/article.php?ModuleId=10005479.

Blockson, Charles L. "Black Samuel Fraunces Patriot, White House Steward and Restaurateur Par Excellence." Temple University Libraries. Accessed February 16, 2012. http://library.temple.edu/collections/blockson/fraunces.jsp;jsessionid=284E5B2DB0413B6C2DEC05D1D0778B5E?bhcp=1

Boisvert, Jayne. "Colonial Hell and Female Resistance in Saint-Domingue." *Journal of Haitian Studies* 7, no. 1 (spring 2001).

Bouvet, Elisabeth. "Dany Laferriere, 2009 Prix Médicis." rfi. Accessed January 4, 2012. http://www.rfi.fr/contenu/20091104-dany-laferriere-prix-medicis-2009.

Boyce Davies, Carole. *Encyclopedia of the African Diaspora: Origins, Experiences, and Culture,* vol. 1, A–C. Santa Barbara, CA: ABC-CLIO, 2008.

Boyd, Herb. "Black Inventors—Past and Present." *The Network Journal,* March 30, 2011. Accessed July 24, 2012. http://www.tnj.com/news/black-american/black-inventors%E2%80%94past-and-present-0.

Brewers Association Presents World Beer Cup 2000 Winner List. Accessed on February 15, 2011. http://www.worldbeercup.org/pdf/2000_winners.pdf.

Brinkmann, Susan. "Celebrating Black History Month: Relying on Providence: Mother Mary Elizabeth Lange." Accessed October 19, 2006. http://www.cst-phl.com/060223/blackcatholic.html.

Buckley, Gail Lumet. *American Patriots: The Story of Blacks in the Military from the Revolution to Desert Storm.* New York, NY: Random House Trade Paperbacks, 2002.

"Bugatti." Mini.43. Accessed July 31, 2012. http://mini.43.free.fr/bugattiroyales.html).

Cahalan, Susannah. "Dreams of His Father: The Surprising Inspiration Behind Alexandre Dumas' Rollicking Adventures 'The Three Musketeers' and 'Monte Cristo.'" *New York Post*, Sep. 30, 2012. Accessed February 27, 2013. http://search.proquest.com/docview/1081701661?accountid=27899.

"Caribbean American Singer Maxwell in Line for Multiple Soul Train Awards, 2009." *Caribbean Today*. Accessed January 13, 2012. http://search.proquest.com/docview/196934382?accountid=12142.

"Carole M. Berotte Joseph, Ph.D." President's Bio from Massachusetts Bay Community College. Accessed January 24, 2011. http://www.massbay.edu/AboutUs/PresidentsOffice/PresidentsBio.aspx.

"Dr. Carole M. Berotte-Joseph First Haitian-American to Head Community College," *New York Carib News* XXVI, no. 1247 (September 26, 2006): 51.

CIA: Haiti, The World FactBook. https://www.cia.gov/library/publications/the-world-factbook/geos/ha.html.

Chapman, Ben. "Haitian Immigrant-filled Robotics Team Earns Contest Berth with Winning Robot." *NY Daily News*, Tuesday, March 22, 2011. Accessed January 29, 2013. http://www.nydailynews.com/new-york/brooklyn/haitian-immigrant-filled-robotics-team-earns-contest-berth-winning-robot-article-1.120339.

"Charles Terres Weymann 1889–1976, AKA Charles II Weymann." Accessed July 24, 2012. http://earlyaviators.com/eweymann.htm.

Charlotin, Manolia. "Anténor Firmin's Work Resonates at NAACP Centennial." *Boston Haitian Reporter*, October 12, 2011. Accessed January 4, 2012. http://www.bostonhaitian.com/node/621.

"Charles Philip Lazarus," *Jamaican History*. Accessed March 31, 2011. http://joyousjam2.tripod.com/charleslazarus/index.html.

"Charles P. Lazarus," *Jamaican History* (February 2004). Accessed March 31, 2011. http://www.joyousjam.info/jamaicanhistoryfebruary2004/id31. html.

"The Charming and Photogenic Michaëlle Jean (27th Governor General of Canada)." Accessed February 16, 2011. http:// hubpages.com/hub/The-charming-and-photogenic-Michalle-Jean-27th-Governor-General-of-Canada

Chaudenson, Robert. *Creolization of Language and Culture*. London, UK: Routledge, 2001.

Cheney, David M. "Bishop Guy A. Sansaricq Auxiliary Bishop Emeritus of Brooklyn, New York, Titular Bishop of Glenndálocha." *Catholic Hierarchy*. Accessed February 15, 2013. http://www. catholic-hierarchy.org/bishop/bsansg.html.

Cho, Nancy. "Savary, Joseph (?–1800s)." Blackpast.org. Accessed February 27, 2013. http://www.blackpast.org/?q=aah/savary-joseph.

Clark, George P. "The Role of the Haitian Volunteers at Savannah in 1779: An Attempt at an Objective View," *Phylon (1960–)* 41, no. 4 (4th Qtr., 1980).

Cobb, Ruth. *History & Mystery: Wall Art in Downtown Bloomington (Who are these people, and why are they on the wall?).* b-n.com. Accessed December 10, 2008. http://www.b-n.com/pages/bsWallArtdwtnBlm.html.

Corbett, Bob. Haiti Section: "Heads of States of Haiti: Presidents, King and Emperors." Accessed April 23, 2015. http://www2.webster.edu/~corbetre/haiti/misctopic/leftover/headstate.htm.

Corbett, Bob. "Notes on Joseph-Antenor Firmin." Webster University. Accessed January 4, 2012. http://www.webster.edu/~corbetre/haiti/history/1844-1915/firmin.htm.

Cross, Allison. "In her five-year term, Michaelle Jean snacked on seal and prorogued Parliament — twice," *The Gazette* montrealgazette.com, July 8, 2010. Accessed February 16, 2011. http://www.montrealgazette.com/life/five+year+term+Michaelle+Jean+snacked+seal+prorogued+Parliament+twice/3250346/story.html.

Crowe, Steve. "Mary Ellen Pleasant: Unsung Heroine." *The New Crisis* 16, no. 1 (January/February 1999): 35.

Dr. Carew, Jan. *Rape of Paradise, Columbus and the Birth of Racism in the Americas.* Brooklyn, New York: A&B Books Publishers, 1994.

Curriculum Initiatives (CCI). Accessed February 16, 2012. http://maap.columbia.edu/place/3.html.

Daggett, Melissa. "Henry Louise Rey, Spiritualism, and Creoles of Color in Nineteenth-Century New Orleans." University of New Orleans Theses and Dissertations. Paper 994, 2009, p. 3. Accessed February 21, 2013. http://scholarworks.uno.edu/cgi/viewcontent.cgi?article=1975&context=td.

Davis, Burke, foreword by Brooke, Edward W. *Black Heroes of the American Revolution*. New York: Harcourt Brace & Company, 1996.

Dayan, Joan. *Haiti, History, and the Gods*. Berkeley: University of California Press, 1995.

Deggs, Mary Bernard, Gould, Virginia Meacham, and Nolan, Charles E. *No Cross, No Crown: Black Nuns in Nineteenth-Century New Orleans*. Bloomington: Indiana University Press, 2001.

De Las Casas, Bartolomé. *The Devastation of the Indies: A Brief Account*, trans. from Spanish by Herma Briffault. Baltimore: John Hopkins University Press, 1992.
http://www.rastaspeaks.com/articles/15122003.html

De Las Casas, Bartolomé. *A Short Account of the Destruction of the Indies,* edited and translated by Nigel Griffin with an introduction by Anthony Pagden. London: Penguin Group, 1992.

DiscoverHaiti. "Jean-Jacques Dessalines: 1758–1806—Hero or Tyrant? Part 1." *History.*
Accessed May 14, 2008. http://www.discoverhaiti.com/history00_10_1.htm.

"Dominican-Haitian Activist Sonia Pierre Dies at 48," *Boston Haitian Reporter*, December 5, 2011. Associated Press. Accessed December 22, 2011.
http://www.bostonhaitian.com/2011/dominican-haitian-activist-sonia-pierre-dies-48.

Desch-Obi, T. J. "Peinillas and Popular Participation: Machete Fighting in Haiti, Cuba and Colombia Memorias." *Revista Digital de Historia y Arqueología desde el Caribe* 6, núm. 11 (Noviembre-sin mes 2009): 144–172; Universidad del Norte Colombia, 147.

Accessed February 28, 2013. http://redalyc.uaemex.mx/src/inicio/ArtPdfRed.jsp?iCve=85512905010.

Desch-Obi, M. Thomas J. *Fighting for Honor: The History of African Martial Art Traditions in the Atlantic World.* Columbia, SC: University of South Carolina Press, 2008.

DesRoches, Reginald, Mary Comerio, Marc Eberhard, Walter Mooney, and Glenn J. Rix.

Dorsey, Joseph. "du Sable, Jean-Baptiste Pointe (1745–1818)." *Encyclopedia of the African Diaspora: Origins, Experiences and Culture.* Editor Carole Boyce-Davies. Santa Barbara, CA: ABC-CLIO, 2007.

DuBois, William Edward Burghardt. *The Autobiography of W. E. B. DuBois.* New York: International Publishers, 1971.

Dubois, Laurent. *Avengers of the New World: The Story of the Haitian Revolution.* Cambridge, Massachusetts, Harvard University Press, 2004.

Dubois, Laurent and Garrigus, John D. *Slave Revolution in the Caribbean, 1789–1804: A Brief History with Documents* Boston, MA; New York, NY: Bedford/St. Martins, 2006.

Dunkel, Greg. "Haitian History: What U.S. Textbooks Don't Tell," *Haiti Progress, This Week in Haiti* 21, no. 27 (September 17–23, 2003). Accessed January 6, 2012. http://www.hartford-hwp.com/archives/43a/549.html.

Dunkel, Greg. "Voodoo and Haiti's Impact on the U.S." *Haiti Progrès Newsweekly* ["This Week in Haiti" is the English section] 21, no. 20 (July 30–August 6, 2003). Accessed May 14, 2010. https://

groups.google.com/forum/?fromgroups=#!topic/misc.activism. progressive/LyTwj6b3FdY

Earle, Alice Morse. *Stage-coach and Tavern Days.* New York: Macmillan Co., 1900.

Economic Times. Accessed July 31, 2012. http://economictimes.indiatimes.com/topic/ Charles-Terres-Weymann/photos.

The Editor. "Contemporary African-American Inventors." Madame Noire, January 10, 2011. Accessed July 24, 2012. http://madamenoire.com/106958/ contemporary-african-americans-inventors/.

Edmond Jr., Alfred. "UBR Spotlight: Meet Successful Teen CEO Leanna Archer." Black Enterprise. Accessed January 29, 2013. http://www.blackenterprise.com/small-business/ ubr-spotlight-meet-successful-teen-ceo-leanna-archer/.

Embassy of the Republic of Haiti. "Key Dates in Haiti's History." Accessed January 30, 2015. http://www.haiti.org/index.php/ economic-xm-affairs-xm.

Evans, Dina. "Barbancourt." Webster University home page of Bob Corbett. Accessed February 15, 2011. http://www.webster. edu/~corbetre/haiti/misctopic/leftover/rhum.htm.

"Eugene Jacques Bullard." National Museum of the USAF. Accessed February 16, 2011. http://www.nationalmuseum.af.mil/factsheets/factsheet. asp?id=705.

"Exterior Memorial Design for African Burial Ground." *Rangel Bulletin: Charles Rangel Congressman, 15ᵗʰ District* 1, no. 2 (May 2005). Accessed October 12, 2007. http://www.house.gov/rangel/bulletin_may2005.html.

"15 Beauties in Miss Universe Spotlight." *Spokesman-Review*, July 15, 1962. Accessed March 31, 2011. http://news.google.com/new spapers?id=504pAAAAIBAJ&sjid=vOcDAAAAIBAJ&pg=530 1,4829544&dq=evelyn-miot&hl=en.

Famous Canadian Women's Famous Firsts. Accessed February 16, 2011. http://www.famouscanadianwomen.com/famous%20firsts/ politicians%20and%20public%20servants.htm.

Femmes d'Haiti, 2005: "Henriett Saint-Marc," Femme Célèbres. Accessed May 14, 2008. http://www.haiticulture.ch/.

Fick, Carolyn E. *The Making of Haiti: The Saint Domingue Revolution from Below*. Knoxville: University of Tennessee Press, 1990.

"First Haitian Illinois State Senator: Haitian Immigrant's Son Kwame Raoul to replace Barack Obama in Illinois Dec 13, 2004." Accessed December 14, 2004. http://haitixchange.com/hx/article.asp?article_id=31&index=0.

Fleming, Beatrice J., and Marion J. Pryde. *Distinguished Negroes Abroad*. Washington, DC: Associated Publishers, 1946.

Fluehr-Lobban, Carolyn. "Antenor Firmin Predicted America's First Black President in 1885!" *University of Illinois Press*, January 23, 2009. Accessed January 4, 2012. http://www.press.uillinois.edu/ wordpress/?p=2136.

Foote, Thelma Wills. *Black and White Manhattan: The History of Racial Formation in Colonial New York City.* New York: Oxford University Press, 2004.

Franciscan University of Steubenville. Accessed October 20, 2006. http://www.bcimall.org/calendar/franuniv/henriette_delille.htm.

Francone, B. "Service of Family Member Makes National History: Grave Marker Honors Haitian-American's Participation in Civil War." *Savannah Morning News*, Nov. 12, 2007. Accessed February 5, 2013. http://search.proquest.com/docview/381955130?accountid=27899.

Frank, Andrew. *The Birth of Black America: The Age of Discovery and The Slave Trade.* New York: Chelsea House Publishers, 1996.

"Fraunces Tavern," MAAP produced by the Columbia Center for New Media Teaching and Learning (CCNMTL) in partnership with Columbia University's Teachers College and Creative. Garcelle Beauvais Biography. Starpluse.com. Accessed January 13, 2012. http://www.starpulse.com/Actresses/Beauvais,_Garcelle/Biography/.

"Fraunces Tavern Historical Landmark." Historical Makers. ExplorePAhistory.com. Accessed February 16, 2012. http://explorepahistory.com/hmarker.php?markerId=1-A-28A.

"French Military Units." W3R [Washington-Rochambeau Revolutionary Route]. Accessed March 22, 2013. http://www.w3r-us.org/history/milu-fr.htm.

Garger, Kenneth. "Got What it Takes." *New York Post*, November 27, 2012. Accessed January 29, 2013. http://www.nypost.com/p/news/local/brooklyn/got_what_it_takes_p5kiqbsAQAEFGQcjNFcYGI

Garner, Carla W. "Bullard, Eugene Jacques (1894–1961)." Blackpast. com. Accessed February 16, 2011. http://www.blackpast.org/?q=aah/bullard-eugene -jacques-1894-1961.

Garrigus, John. "Haiti Independence Revolution," *Revolutionary Movement in World History From 1750 to the Present,* vol. 2, H–P. Santa Barbara, California: ABC CLIO, 2006.

Geggus, David. "The British Government and The Saint Domingue Slave Revolt, 1791–1793," *The English Historical Review* 96 no. 379 (April 1981): 285–305.

Girard, Philippe R. *Haiti: The Tumultuous History—From Pearl of the Caribbean to Broken Nation.* New York: Palgrave Macmillan, 2010.

Goodwin, Stefan. *Interdependencies, Relocations, and Globalization.* Lanham, MD: Lexington Books, 2009.

"Gov. Gen. Jean Gets 21-gun Salute." CBC News, September 29, 2010. Accessed February 16, 2011. http://www.cbc.ca/canada/ story/2010/09/29/govenor-general-saluted-929.html.

Graves, Kerry A. *Haiti.* Mankato, Minnesota: Bridgestone Books, 2002.

Green, Thomas A. *Martial Arts in the Modern World.* Westport, CT: Praeger, 2003.

The Habari Network. "Profile: Leanna Archer, Fouunder and CEO of Leanna's Inc." Accessed January 29, 2013. http://www. thehabarinetwork.com/profile-leanna-archer-founder-and-ceo- of-leanna%E2%80%99s-inc.

"Haiti: One Year Later," Whitehouse Blog posted by Patrick Gaspard, January 12, 2011. Accessed December 22, 2011. http://www.whitehouse.gov/blog/2011/01/12/haiti-one-year-later.

"Haiti History 101." The Haitian Tuskegee Airmen. Accessed July 24, 2012. http://kreyolicious.com/haiti-history-101-the-haitian -tuskegee-airmen/1597/.

"Haitian American Designer Helps Open African Burial Ground." HardbeatNews.Com. *Daily Caribbean Diaspora*, October 12, 2007. Accessed October 12, 2007. http://www.hardbeatnews.com/editor/RTE/my_documents/my_ files/details.asp?newsid=13820&title=Top%20Stories.

"Haitian-Born Laferriere, the First Canadian Writer to Win France's Prestigious Medicis Literary Prize." November 4, 2009. Accessed January 4, 2012. http://www.wehaitians.com/dany%20laferriere%20wins%20 medcis%20literary%20prize.html.

Haitian Historical and Cultural Legacy: A Journey Through Time: A Resource Guide for Teachers, HABETAC The Haitian Bilingual/ ESL Technical Assistance Center, 1–2. Accessed March 12, 2012. http://depthome.brooklyn.cuny.edu/habetac/Publications_files/ Haitian-Historical.pdf.

"Haitian Immigration: Eighteenth and Nineteenth Centuries." Schomburg Center for Research in Black Culture, the New York Public Library. Accessed February 27, 2013. http://www.inmotionaame.org/print. cfm;jsessionid=f830178511361544584816?migration=5&bhcp=1.

Hall, Michael R. *Historical Dictionary of Haiti*. Lanham: Scarecrow Press, 2012.

Harris, Leslie M. *In the Shadow of Slavery: African Americans in New York City, 1626–1863*. Chicago: University of Chicago Press, 2003. Accessed February 25, 2013. http://hdl.handle.net/2027/heb.06703.

Heinl, Robert Debs, and Heinl, Nancy Gordon. *Written in Blood*. Lanham: University Press of America, 2005.

Henry, Guy, and Hershey, Clair. "Cassava in South America and the Caribbean." *CAB International*, 2002 *Cassava: Biology, Production and Utilization*. http://www.ciat.cgiar.org/downloads/pdf/cabi_05ch2.pdf.

Hewitt, Lawrence L., and Arthur W. Bergeron. *Louisianians in the Civil War*. Columbia: University of Missouri Press, 2002. Accessed February 21, 2013. http://search.ebscohost.com/login.aspx?direct=true&scope=site&db=nlebk&db=nlabk&AN=113912

Hochschild, Adam. "Birth of a Nation: Has the Bloody 200-year History of Haiti Doomed It to More Violence?" *San Francisco Chronicle*, Sunday, May 30, 2004. Accessed December 20, 2006. http://sfgate.com/cgibin/article.cgi?file=/chronicle/archive/2004/05/30/CMGKG6F3UV1.DTL.

"Honoring Samuel Fraunces at St. Peter's, June 26, 2010," The President's House in Philadelphia. Accessed February 16, 2012. http://www.ushistory.org/presidentshouse/history/frauncesobelisk.htm.

Hoobler, Thomas and Dorothy. *Toussaint Louverture*. New York: Chelsea House Publishers, 1990.

Horton, James Oliver, and Lois E. Horton. *Slavery and the Making of America*. New York: Oxford University Press, 2004.

Hudson, Christopher. "The French Fuhrer: Genocidal Napoleon was as Barbaric as Hitler, Historian Claims." *Daily Mail*, July 24, 2008. Accessed March 12, 2012. http://www.dailymail.co.uk/news/article-1038453/The-French-Fuhrer-Genocidal-Napoleon-barbaric-Hitler-historian-claims.html#ixzz2McmaOv1T.

Hughes, Zondra. "What Happened to the Only Black Family on the Titanic." *Ebony* LV, no. 8, (June 2000): 148–150.

Hunt, Alfred N. *Haiti's Influence on Antebellum America; Slumbering Volcano in the Caribbean.* Baton Rouge: Louisiana State University Press, 1988.

James, C. L. R. *The Black Jacobins: Toussaint Louverture and The San Domingo Revolution.* New York: Vintage Books, 1989.

Jean-Charles, Georges. *Dictionnaire Historique de la Révolution Haïtienne (1789–1804).* Montréal, Québec: Éditions Images; Éditions du CIDIHCA, 2003.

Jean-Louis, Nicole. *History and Culture of Haiti: Journey Through Visual Art.* Xlibris Corporation, 2012.

Jet. "Marjorie Vincent, former Miss America, named TV anchor in Meridian, MS—for NBC-affiliate WGBC-TV—Brief Article," *Jet* 85, no. 6 (Dec. 6, 1993).

Johnston, Harry Hamilton. *The Negro in the New World.* London: Macmillan, 1910.

Jones, Nigel. "The Black Count: Glory, Revolution, Betrayal and the Real Count of Monte Cristo by Tom Reiss—review." *The Guardian*, Friday, September 28, 2012. Accessed February 27, 2013. http://www.guardian.co.uk/books/2012/sep/28/black-count-tom-reiss-review.

Juste, André. "Haiti." *Africana: The Encyclopedia of the African and African American Experience.* New York: Basic Civitas Books, 2005.

Kerns, Fleurimond W. "The Haitian Flag—Birth of a Symbol," translated by Greg Dunkel
May 18, 2003 from International Action Center. Accessed January 6, 2012.
http://www.iacenter.org/haiti/flag.htm.

Ketner, Joseph D., and Robert S. Duncanson. *The Emergence of the African-American Artist: Robert S. Duncanson, 1821–1872.* Columbia: University of Missouri Press, 1993.

Knight, Franklin W., 1990: *The Caribbean* (New York: Oxford University Press).

Laguerre, Michel S. *American Odyssey: Haitians in New York City.* Ithaca, NY: Cornell University Press, 1984.

Lawless, Robert. *Haiti's Bad Press.* Rochester, Vermont: Schenkman Books, Inc., 1992.

Leger, Jacques Nicolas. *Haiti Her History and Her Detractors.* Westport, Connecticut: Negro Universities Press, 1970.

Lewis, Jone Johnson. "Henriette Delille." Women's History. About. com. Accessed October 20, 2006. http://womenshistory.about. com/od/romancatholicchurch/p/h_delille.htm.

Lies, Anne. *The Earthquake in Haiti.* Edina, Minn: ABDO Pub., 2011.

"Lincoln Poems." Millikin University. Accessed December 10, 2008. https://www.millikin.edu/english/Guillory'sWeb/www/Lincolnpoems.html.

"Lincoln Poems," Millikin University and Harris, Kathryn M. "Generations of Pride: African American Timeline: A Selected Chronology." Illinois Historic Preservation Agency from the Abraham Lincoln Presidential Library. Accessed December 10, 2008. http://www.illinoishistory.gov/lib/GenPrideAfAm.htm.

"Lincoln Poems," Millikin University and Krohe, James. *Honest Abe's Honest Almanac: Being a Cornucopia of Amazing Facts, Useful Wisdom, and Amusing Anecdotes Concerning the Social, Political, Economic, Recreational, Educational, and Cultural Life of Springfield, Illinois, Past and Present.* Springfield, IL: Talisman Press, 1974. Accessed December 10, 2008. http://www.archive.org/details/honestabeshonest00kroh.

Loewen, James W. *Lies My Teacher Told Me: Everything Your American History Textbook Got Wrong.* New York: New Press, 2008. Accessed May 14, 2010. http://public.eblib.com/EBLPublic/PublicView.do?ptiID=579047.

Lowery, Woodbury. *The Spanish Settlements Within the Present Limits of the United States, 1513–1561.* New York: Russell & Russell, Inc., 1959.

MAAP (Mapping the African American Past). "Pierre Toussaint." Accessed February 15, 2013. http://maap.columbia.edu/place/13.html.

Mackey, Doug. "Mattawa's Dr. Firmin Monestime Remembered." Community Voices, *[Heritage Perspectives],* October 26, 2007. Accessed January 4, 2012. http://www.pastforward.ca/perspectives/columns/07_10_26.htm.

Marcus, Lilit. "Miss Haiti: Is Having a National Beauty Queen an Accomplishment?" *Huffington Post* online, August 20, 2010. Accessed January 10, 2012.

http://www.huffingtonpost.com/lilit-marcus/miss-haiti-is-having-a-na_b_687151.html.

Marian Community Hospital. "Mother Theresa Maxis Duchemin." Maxis Foundation. Accessed October 23, 2006. http://www.marianhospital.org/services/maxis.php.

McClarey, Donald R. "Venerable Pierre Toussaint." *The American Catholic.* Accessed February 15, 2013. http://the-american-catholic.com/2010/05/21/venerable-pierre-toussaint/.

McClendon III, John H. "Reason, Charles Lewis (1818–1893)." Blackpast.org. Accessed December 12, 2011. http://www.blackpast.org/?q=aah/reason-charles-lewis-1818-1893.

McNamara, Pat. "Edmonia Lewis: Artist, Woman of Color, Catholic as a Black Catholic artist, Lewis brought a uniquely African perspective to her religious work." *Patheos Catholic* [Catholic Channel Section], November 01, 2010. Accessed March 13, 2013. http://www.patheos.com/Resources/Additional-Resources/Edmonia-Lewis-Artist-Woman-of-Color-Catholic.html.

Meade, Teresa A. *A History of Modern Latin America, 1800–2000.* Oxford: Blackwell, 2008.

"Michaëlle Jean." *The Canadian Encyclopedia.* Accessed February 16, 2011.
http://www.thecanadianencyclopedia.com/index.cfm?PgNm=TCE&Params=A1ARTA0009825#ArticleContents.

Mike F. Molaire Biography, Amazon.com (information for the biography was provided by the author or his representative). Accessed July 25, 2012. http://www.amazon.com/Mike-F.-Molaire/e/B005XRWLPW.

Moitt, Bernard. *Women and Slavery in the French Antilles, 1635–1848*. Indiana University Press, 2001.

Mother Mary Elizabeth Lange, OSP. Accessed October 19, 2006. http://www.oblatesisters.com/page20.html.

In Motion: The African-American Migration Experience. "The Haitian Influence on Religion." Accessed October 20, 2006. http://www.inmotionaame.org/migrations/topic_body.cfm?migration=5&topic=7.

Myers, Jacob W. "History of the Gallatin Salines." *Journal of the Illinois State Historical Society*, June 9, 2003. Accessed October 14, 2007. http://www.illinoishistory.com/1922-gallatinsalines.html

Montanaro, Domenico. "Gaspard Named WH Political Director." *FirstRead*, MSNBC News online, Nov. 21, 2008. Accessed December 2, 2008. http://firstread.msnbc.msn.com/archive/2008/11/21/1685663.aspx.

Neal, Anthony W. "Boston's Black Medical Community Thrived in the Mid-19th Century." *The Bay State Banner.* Accessed February 25, 2013. http://www.baystatebanner.com/local13-2012-04-12.

Miss New York TEEN USA 2011 Crowning Moments.mp4. Uploaded by blackwatervideo on Dec 3, 2010. Accessed March 31, 2011. http://www.youtube.com/watch?v=0jx-KzUFTgk.

"New York opens slave burial site: A burial ground for African slaves, which had been forgotten for almost two centuries, has been opened to the public in New York." *BBC News International Version*, October 6, 2007. Accessed October 12, 2007. http://news.bbc.co.uk/2/hi/americas/7031142.stm.

Nirit Ben-Ari, Ha'aretz. "Haiti and the Jews: Forgotten History." Translation: Pacha Dovinsky, from *World War 4 Report*, February 1, 2010 [Nirit Ben-Ari is a doctoral student in political science who teaches at Israel's Sapir College. This article first appeared in Hebrew in the Israeli daily *Ha'aretz* on Jan. 22]. Accessed January 4, 2012. http://ww4report.com/node/8272.

NgCheong-Lum, Roseline, and Leslie Jermyn. *Haiti*. New York: Marshall Cavendish Benchmark, 2006.

Norment, Lynn. "Back-to-Back Black Miss Americas: Marjorie Judith Vincent Makes History When Crowned by Reigning Black Queen," *Ebony* XLVI, no. 2 (December 1990): 46–50.

Onofre, Alejandro Guevara: "Haiti: The First Black Republic in the History." Accessed March 31, 2011. http://www.voiceofarkansas.com/content/p/5031/catid/36/artid/3159.

Onofre, Alejandro Guevara. "Miss Universe 2007 in Mexico is a profile about Miss Universe Pageant. In my opinion, I think that Miss Universe Pageant is a symbol of the modern woman in this century …" Buzzle.com. Accessed March 31, 2011. http://www.buzzle.com/articles/miss-universe-2007-mexico.html.

"Overview of the 2010 Haiti Earthquake." *Earthquake Spectra* 27, no. 1 (October 2011): S1-S21. Accessed January 30, 2015. http://escweb.wr.usgs.gov/share/mooney/142.pdf.

Pamphile, Leon D. *Haitians and African Americans*. Gainesville: University Press of Florida, 2001. Accessed March 7, 2013. http://public.eblib.com/EBLPublic/PublicView.do?ptiID=290214.

Paquin, Raphaël, and Brax, José (eds.). *History of Haiti 1492–2000 in French and English*. Pétion-Ville, Haiti: Sogebel, 2002.

Paravisini-Gebert, Lizabeth. *Literature of the Caribbean*. Westport, CT: Greenwood Press, 2008.

"Patrick Gaspard." DiscovertheNetworks.org. Accessed December 22, 2011.
http://www.discoverthenetworks.org/individualProfile.asp?indid=2420.

Pearson, Jake. "Daughter of Haitian Immigrants Vying to be 1st Miss Teen USA from N.Y in 30 yrs. Crown Would Be a Thing of Beauty," *New York Daily News,* Tuesday March 29, 2011, 6.

Perusse, Roland I. *Historical Dictionary of Haiti*. Metuchen, NJ: Scarecrow Press, Inc., 1977.

Pickett, Mary. "Samuel W. Lewis: Orphan leaves mark on Bozeman," *The Gazette* Staff, March 1, 2002. Accessed March 13, 2013.
http://billingsgazette.com/lifestyles/samuel-w-lewis-orphan-leaves-mark-on-bozeman/article_bf7abce6-bbf5-5fe2-8269-d891f9e0682a.html#ixzz2NT4NPYSA.

Pierre-Pierre, Garry. "Dr. Carole Berotte Joseph Named President of Bronx Community College." *Haitian Times.* Accessed December 29, 2011.
http://haitiantimes.com/view/full_story/11122431/article-Dr--Carole-Berotte-Joseph-Named-President-of-Bronx-Community-College.

The Q: the Side Quddus' Official Website. Accessed January 13, 2012.
http://www.theqside.com/about-2.

"Quebec, Canada, 28th International Conference on Digital Printing Technologies, Society for Imaging Science & Technology," Linkedin. Accessed July 25, 2012.
http://events.linkedin.com/nip-28-short-course-1053541.

"Raymond Cassagnol." fordi9.com. Accessed July 24, 2012. http://www.fordi9.com/Pages/AffairCassagnol.htm.

Reinhardt, Catherine. "Heroine Maroon Slave." *Revolutionary Freedoms: A History of Survival, Strength and Imagination in Haiti*. Caribbean Studies Press, Imprint of Educa vision Inc., 2006.

"Reserve." Rhum Barbancourt. Accessed on February 15, 2011. http://www.barbancourt.net/rhum-barbancourt-reserve-du-domaine.php?langue=en.

Rhum Barbancourt. Accessed February 15, 2011. http://www.barbancourt.net/index2.php?mode=1&langue=en.

Robinson, Randle. *An Unbroken Agony: Haiti, From Revolution to the Kidnapping of a President*. New York: A Member of the Perseus Books Group, 2007.

Roc, François. *Dictionnaire de la Révolution Haïtienne, 1789-1804: Dictionnaire des Evénements, des Emblèmes et Devises, des Institutions et Actes, des Leux et des Personnages*. Montréal: Éditions Guildives, 2006.

Rodman, Selden. *Haiti the Black Republic The Standard Guide to Haiti*. Old Greenwich: Devin-Adair, Publishers, 1984.

Rodney Leon, AIA, NOMA, AARRIS Architects. Accessed October 3, 2007. http://www.aarris.com/.

"Rodney Leon Tapped to Design Memorial for National Historic Landmark Winner to Create Memorial for 17th, 18th-Century Africans." US General Service Administration, Friday, April 29, 2005. Accessed October 3, 2007.

http://www.africanburialground.gov/Press_Releases/ rodneyleon_042905.pdf.

Rogers, J. A. *World's Great Men of Color,* vol. 2. New York: A Touchstone Book, 1996.

Rogers, J. A. *100 Amazing Facts About the Negro with Complete Proof.* New York: H. M. Rogers, 1995.

Rogers, J. A. *Your History: From the Beginning of Time to the Present.* Baltimore, MD: Black Classic Press, 1989.

Rogers, J. A. *Sex and Race, Volume 2: The New World.* United States, 1967.

Rogers, J. A. *Africa's Gift to America: The Afro-American in the Making and Saving of the United States. With New Supplement: Africa and Its Potentialities.* New York: H. M. Rogers, 1961.

Ros, Martin. *Night of Fire the Black Napoleon and the Battle for Haiti.* United States: Da Capo Press, 1994.

Rouse, Irving. *The Tainos Rise & Decline of the People Who Greeted Columbus.* New Haven: Yale University Press, 1992.

Rulers.org. "Counttried and Territories (H)." Accessed April 23, 2015. http://rulers.org/index.html.

Salisbury, Stephan. "At. Last, Honoring the Burial Site of 'Black Sam.'" Philly.com, June 25, 2010. Accessed February 16, 2012. http://articles.philly.com/2010-06-25/news/24966504_ 1_burial-site-racial-identity-descendants.

"Sarodj Bertin." Haitian American Community Association. Accessed January 10, 2012.

http://www.hacachicago.com/index.php?option=com_content&view=article&id=217.

Scott, Lawrence P., and William M. Womack. *Double V: The Civil Rights Struggle of the Tuskegee Airmen.* East Lansing, MI: Michigan State University Press, 1998. Accessed July 24, 2012. http://search.ebscohost.com/login.aspx?direct=true&scope=site&db=nlebk&db=nlabk&AN=22823.

Séjour, Victor, and Norman R. Shapiro. *The Fortune-teller.* Urbana: University of Illinois Press, 2002.

Sellers, W. F. Burton. "Heroes of Haiti." January 11, 1999. Accessed April 24, 2008. http://www.hartford-hwp.com/archives/43a/168.html.

Simonelli, Frederick J. *The Historical Encyclopedia of World Slavery,* vol. 1, A–K. Santa Barbara, CA: ABC-CLIO, 1997.

Sisters, Servants of the Immaculate Heart of Mary. "Mother Theresa Maxis Duchemin." IHM Founder. Accessed October 23, 2006. http://www.ihmimmaculata.org/history/founder.html.

Sluby, Patricia Carter. *The Inventive Spirit of African Americans: Patented Ingenuity.* Westport, CT: Praeger, 2004.

Smith, Phyllis. *Bozeman and the Gallatin Valley: A History.* Helena, Montana: Falcon Press Publ., 1996.

St. Augustine Catholic Church of New Orleans. "Events." Chronology of Church History. Accessed October 20, 2006. http://www.staugustinecatholicchurch-neworleans.org/hist-chron.htm.

Stephens, George E., and Yacovone, Donald. *A Voice of Thunder: A Black Soldier's Civil War.* Urbana: University of Illinois Press, 1998.

Stewart, Jeffrey C. *1001 Things Everyone Should Know about African American History.* New York: Gramercy Books, 2006.

Sylvain, Patrick. "Ertha Pascal-Trouillot: Unsung Heroine of Democracy." *Boston Haitian Reporter*, March 14, 2011. Accessed January 4, 2012. http://www.bostonhaitian.com/node/411.

Taft, Edna. *A Puritan in Voodoo-Land.* Philadelphia: Penn Pub. Co., 1938.

Truck, Mary C. *Haiti, Land of Inequality.* Minneapolis: Lerner Publication Company, 1999.

Tucker, Spencer. *A Global Chronology of Conflict: From the Ancient World to the Modern Middle East.* Santa Barbara, CA: ABC-CLIO, 2010.

"Tuskegee Airmen Pilot Listing." Tuskegee University. Accessed July 24, 2012. http://kreyolicious.com/haiti-history-101-the-haitian-tuskegee-airmen/1597/.

"Tyrone Edmond." Facebook. Accessed January 13, 2012. http://www.facebook.com/pages/Tyrone-Edmond/103087859730938.

Victor, A. J. *In the Name of Liberty: A History of Haiti (Pre-1492–1806).* Linivè Kreyòl, 2004.

"The Virtual Jewish History Tour Haiti." Jewish Virtual Library. Accessed January 3, 2012. http://www.jewishvirtuallibrary.org/jsource/vjw/haiti.html.

Von Fleischer, Aylmer. *Retake Your Fame: Black Contribution to World Civilization.* Bloomington, Indiana: Authorhouse, 2004.

Watts, Richards. "Dessalines, Jean-Jacques." *Africana: The Encyclopedia of the African and African American Experience*, second edition, vol. 2, Catimbó–Giovanni. Oxford University Press, 2005.

"Weymann-American Body Company, 1926–1932; Indianapolis, Indiana." Coachbuilt. Accessed July 31, 2012. http://www.coachbuilt.com/bui/w/weymann/weymann.htm.

Williams, John A. "Edmond Family's Secret Turns Out to Be Revealing Story," *Newsok* website, November 8, 2008. Accessed December 10, 2008. http://newsok.com/edmond-familys-secret-turns-out-to-be-revealing-story/article/3319937.

Willson, Joseph, and Julie Winch. *The Elite of Our People: Joseph Willson's Sketches of Black Upper-Class Life in Antebellum Philadelphia*. University Park: Pennsylvania State University Press, 2000.

Winsor, Justin. *Narrative and Critical History of America,* vol. 2. Boston, New York, Houghton, Mifflin and Company, 1886.

Woodson, Carter Godwin. *The Negro in Our History*. Washington, DC: Associated Publishers, 1922.

Worth, John E. "History & Archaeology: Spanish Exploration." *New Georgia Encyclopedia*, Oct 17, 2003. Accessed January 9, 2008. http://www.georgiaencyclopedia.org/nge/Article.jsp?id=h-1012.

Wright, R. R. "Negro Companions of the Spanish Explorers." *American Anthropologist*, New Series 4, no. 2 (April–June 1902).

Yu, Karlson. "Springfield Race Riot, 1908." BlackPast.org. Accessed December 10, 2008. http://www.blackpast.org/?q=aah/springfield-race-riot-1908.

Marjorie Charlot

Further Reading

North America's First Slave Revolt

Books

Anderson, Dr. Claud, and Brant Anderson. *More Dirty Little Secrets About Black History, Its Heroes, and Other Troublemakers,* vol. 2. Maryland: PowerNomics Corporation of America, 2006, 29–31.

Aptheker, Herbert. *American Negro Slave Revolts.* New York: Columbia University Press, 1943, 163.

Bennett, Lerone. *Before the Mayflower: A History of the Negro in America, 1619–1962.* Chicago: Johnson Pub. Co., 1962, 101.

Winsor, Justin. *Narrative and Critical History of America,* vol. 2. Boston; New York: Houghton, Mifflin and Company, 1886, 238–241.

Articles

Wright, R. R. "Negro Companions of the Spanish Explorers." *American Anthropologist,* New Series 4, no. 2 (April–June 1902): 217–228.

Wright, R. R. "Negro Companions of the Spanish Explorers." *Phylon (1940–1956)* 2, no. 4 (4th Qtr., 1941): 328–29.

Empress Marie-Claire Heureuse Félicité

To know more on Empress Marie-Claire Heureuse Félicité, see: http://www.youtube.com/watch?v=qEiP3Coy5cQ.

Tuskegee Airmen

Kat. "Haiti History 101: The Haitian Tuskegee Airmen." *Kreyolicious.* June 17, 2015. http://kreyolicious.com/haiti-history-101-the-haitian-tuskegee-airmen/1597/.

"Always Remembering His Dad—A Tuskegee Airman." [This site is dedicated to Ludovic Audant from his son Pierre Audant.] http://www.broward.org/ECountyLine/Pages/Vol_36_no_5/mainStory1.htm.

"Haitian Tuskegee Airmen!" *Lay People United for Jesus.* [This website has information on the airmen along with images and a video.] http://www.hadob.org/newsbriefs_detail.php?newsbriefs_id=27.

"Haitian-Tuskegee Airman Receives Medal—April 6, 2010." [A YouTube video shows Mr. Raymond Cassagnol.] http://www.youtube.com/watch?v=D5WRedReSXQ.

Illustrations

Map of Haiti

Road map of Haiti in French by © Rémi Kaupp: CC-BY-SA, Wikimedia Commons https://commons.wikimedia.org/wiki/File:Haiti_road_map-fr.svg.

Architecture

French Quarters, New Orleans (photos by Marjorie Charlot 2012).

Aerial View of Citadelle Laferrière photo by SPC Gibran Torres, United States Army

(Citadelle Laferrière aerial view from an Army UH-60 Blackhawk during operation Unified Response),
Wikipedia: http://en.wikipedia.org/wiki/Citadelle_Laferri%C3%A8re.

Ironwork, French Quarters, New Orleans (photos by Marjorie Charlot 2012).

The Burial Ground (photos by Marjorie Charlot 2010).

Dumas Family

General Alexandre ("Alexandre the Greatest") Dumas from
Blackpast.org
http://www.blackpast.org/gah/
dumas-thomas-alexandre-1762-1806

Un Héros de Lépopée le général Dumas au pont de clausen from the *Le Petit Journal,* Mai 26, 1912, numéro 1123, Bibliothèque Nationale de France:
http://gallica.bnf.fr/ark:/12148/bpt6k717010x/f8.image

Alexandre Dumas, Père
Davidson, Arthur F. 1902. *Alexandre Dumas (père) his life and works.* Philadelphia: J.B. Lippincott, between pgs.330-331.
https://books.google.com/
books?id=J409AAAAYAAJ&dq=Alexandre%20
Dumas&pg=PP1#v=onepage&q=Alexandre%20
Dumas&f=false

Alexandre Dumas, File
Dole, Nathan Haskell, Forest Morgan, Caroline Ticknor, Donald Grant Mitchell, and Andrew Lang. 1898. *The International library of famous literature: selections from the world's great*

writers *Ancient, Mediæval, and Modern, with Biographical and Explanatory Notes and with Introductions, Volume XVIII.* New York: Merrill and Baker, Between pgs. 8536-8537.
https://books.google.com/
books?id=5yJNAAAAYAAJ&dq=Alexandre%20Dumas%20
camille&pg=PA8271#v=onepage&q=Alexandre%20
Dumas%20camille&f=false

Education

Charles Reason

McClendon III, John H. Reason, Charles Lewis (1818-1893), Blackpast.org
http://www.blackpast.org/aah/reason-charles-lewis-1818-1893

Explorers and Settlers

Jean Baptiste Pointe Du Sable settlement [by A. T. Andreas 1884: *An imaginary view of the site of Chicago in 1779 (Then called Eschikago), showing the cabin of Jean Baptiste Point de Sable (colored) the first permanent settler—see pages 70–72*]
Andreas, A. T. *History of Chicago from the Earliest Period to the Present Time.* Chicago: A. T. Andreas Publisher, 1884, before title page.
http://archive.org/details/historyofchicago01inandr

Haitian Fighting Styles

Stick-Fighting in St. Domingue late eighteenth century

Nicolas Ponce. Recueil des vues des lieux principaux de la colonie Francaise de Saint-Domingue. Paris: A.P.D.R., 1791, plate no. 26.

Negres de St. Domingue se battabtau bâton

Grasset de Saint-Sauveur, Jacques. 1796. *Encyclopédie des voyages, contenant l'abrégé historique des moeurs, usages, habitudes domestiques, religions, fêtes, supplices, funérailles, sciences, arts, et commerce de tous les peuples: et la collection complette de leurs habillemens civils, militaires, religieux et dignitaires, dessinés d'après nature, gravés avec soin et coloriés à l'aquarelle.* ([Paris]: Deroy).

Lewis Family

Mary Edmonia Lewis

Blackpast.org
http://www.blackpast.org/aah/lewis-edmonia-1845

Property of Samuel W. Lewis:

Leeson, M. A. *History of Montana, 1739–1885: a history of its discovery and settlement, social and commercial progress, mines and miners, agriculture and stock-growing, churches, schools and societies, Indians and Indian wars, vigilantes, courts of justice, newspaper press, navigation, railroads and statistics: with histories of counties, cities, villages and mining camps: also, personal reminiscences of great historic value, views characteristic of the territory in our own times, and portraits of pioneers and representative men in the professions and trades.* Chicago: Warner, Beers & Co. 1885, 254.

Military, Revolts, Revolutions, and Wars

America Section

Georges Biassou

Dubroca, Louis, and Juan López Cancelada. 1806. *Vida de J.J. Dessalines, gefe de los negros de Santo Domingo: Con notas muy circunstanciadas sobre el origen, caracter y atrocidades de los principales gefes de aquellos rebeldes desde el principio de la insurreccion en 1791.* México: Zúñiga y Ontiveros, Before cover pages. https://archive.org/details/vidadejjdessalin00dubr

Samuel Fraunces

Earle, Alice Morse. *Stage-coach and Tavern Days.* New York: Macmillan Co., 1900, 184.

Fraunces Tavern at 54 Pearl Street, Manhattan, New York
(Photos by Marjorie Charlot 2010)

Plaque of Fraunces Tavern
(Photos by Marjorie Charlot 2010)

France Section

Jean-Louis Michel
Vigeant, Arsène. 1883, Petit essai historique: un maître d'armes sous la Restauration. http://gallica.bnf.fr/ark:/12148/bpt6k6545612b/f12.item

General Alexandre ("Alexandre the Greatest") Dumas— Commander of Napoleon's Cavalry
Hugo, Abel. *France militaire: histoire des armées françaises de terre et de mer de 1792 à 1837.* Paris: Delloye, 1833, 148–149.

Haiti Section

Bloodhounds Attacking a Black Family in the Woods

Rainsford, Marcus. *An historical account of the black empire of Hayti, comprehending a view of the principal transactions in the revolution of Saint Domingo.* J. Cundee, 1805, 338–339.

The Mode of Training Bloodhounds in St. Domingo and of Exercising them by Chafseur

Rainsford, Marcus. *An historical account of the black empire of Hayti, comprehending a view of the principal transactions in the revolution of Saint Domingo.* J. Cundee, 1805, 422–423.

The Mode of Exterminating the Black Army as Practiced by the French

Rainsford, Marcus. *An historical account of the black empire of Hayti, comprehending a view of the principal transactions in the revolution of Saint Domingo.* J. Cundee, 1805, 326–327.

Combat et Prise de la Crête-à-Pierrot (Fight and Capture of Crête-à-Pierrot)

Norvins, Jacques Marquet de Montbreton de, Horace Vernet, and Denis-Auguste-Marie Raffet. *Histoire de Napoléon.* Bruxelles: Soc. typ. belge Ad. Wahlen & Co., 1839.
Ulises Hereaux was president of Dominican Republic.

Battle at San Domingo by January Suchodolski

Wikipedia: http://en.wikipedia.org/wiki/File:San_Domingo.jpgg. (Public Domain {{PD-US}})

General Alexande Sabes Petion President, 1807

Steward, T. G. *The Haitian Revolution, 1791 to 1804: or, Side lights on the French Revolution.* New York: Crowell, 1915, 258–259.

General Henri Christophe, "King" of Haiti
Steward, T. G. *The Haitian Revolution, 1791 to 1804: or, Side lights on the French Revolution.* New York: Crowell, 1915, 138–139.

Toussaint Louverture
Steward, T. G. *The Haitian Revolution, 1791 to 1804: or, Side lights on the French Revolution.* New York: Crowell, 1915, before title page.

General Jean Jacque Dessalines, Liberator of Haiti

Steward, T. G. *The Haitian Revolution, 1791 to 1804: or, Side lights on the French Revolution.* New York: Crowell, 1915, 154–155.

General Andre Rigaud, Chief of the Mulattoes
Steward, T. G. *The Haitian Revolution, 1791 to 1804: or, Side lights on the French Revolution.* New York: Crowell, 1915, 60–61.

General Jean Pierre Boyer, president
Steward, T. G. *The Haitian Revolution, 1791 to 1804: or, Side lights on the French Revolution.* New York: Crowell, 1915, 194–195.

Adjutant General E. V. Menter, served under Dessalines
Steward, T. G. *The Haitian Revolution, 1791 to 1804: or, Side lights on the French Revolution.* New York: Crowell, 1915, 206–207.

World Wars Section

Eugene Jacques Bullard: The Black Swallow of Death
U.S. Air Force [Air Force Photos]
http://www.af.mil/News/Photos.aspx?igphoto=2000181932

Religion

Henriette Dellile Stained-Glass Window (photos by Marjorie Charlot 2012).

Mother Mary Elizabeth Lange

Photo Credit: Archdiocese of Baltimore. Accessed March 15, 2013. Archdiocese of Baltimore"

http://msa.maryland.gov/megafile/msa/speccol/sc3500/sc3520/013500/013580/html/13580images.html. (Public Domain {{PD-US}})
(This information resource of the Maryland State Archives is presented here for fair use in the public domain. When this material is used, in whole or in part, proper citation and credit must be attributed to the Maryland State Archives.)

Pierre Toussaint

Hannah Farnham Sawyer Lee, 1780–1865, *Memoir of Pierre Toussaint, Born a Slave in St. Domingo.* Boston: Crosby, Nichols, and Company, 1854.
http://docsouth.unc.edu/neh/leehf/frontis.html

Scholars and Writers

Joseph Auguste Anténor Firmin

Wikipedia: "Anténor Firmin," Litterature, Lehman
http://www.lehman.cuny.edu/ile.en.ile/paroles/firmin.html

Index

- T -

Titanic, 106, 107
Toussaint, Pierre, 118-119
Toussaint, Rose-Marie, 57
traditional African religion, 121
Tuskegee Airmen, xii, 99
Tuskegee Institute, 99, 100

- U -

U.S. (United States), 60, 61, 96, 101
Underground Railroad, 30
Union Army, 66

- V -

Venezuela, xi, 85, 98

Vincent, Marjorie Judith, 28
Virginia, 30, 36, 67, 68, 82

- W -

War of 1812, 64-66
Washington, George, xi, 61, 62, 85, 96
Weymann, Charles Terres, 110-111
Women, xii, 12, 14, 45, 72, 73, 77, 81,
        82, 83, 108, 116, 117, 119, 120
women fighters, 81
World War I, 98
World War II, 99

- Y -

Yorktown, 60

Printed in the United States
By Bookmasters